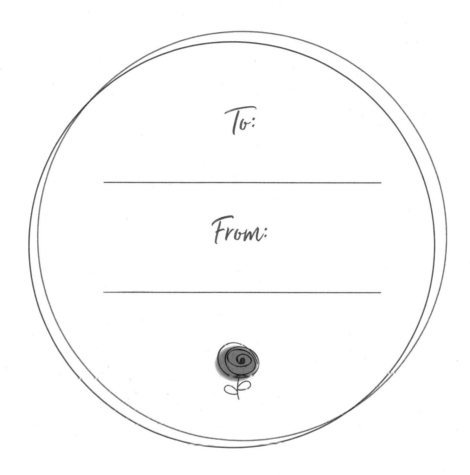

To:

_____

From:

_____

BECKY THOMPSON

Author of *Hope Unfolding*

Truth Unchanging

Hearing God Daily in the Midst of Motherhood

— *Grace-Filled Devotions* —

in 5 Minutes or Less

WATERBROOK

Hardcover ISBN 978-0-525-65229-8
eBook ISBN 978-0-525-65247-2

Copyright © 2019 by Rebecca F. Thompson
Illustrations © 2019 by Shutterstock and Freepik

Cover design by Becky Thompson and Karen Sherry; cover image by Stephanie Studer
Interior design by Karen Sherry

The author is represented by Alive Literary Agency, 7680 Goddard Street, Suite 200, Colorado Springs, CO 80920, www.aliveliterary.com.

Published in the United States by WaterBrook, an imprint of the Crown Publishing Group, a division of Penguin Random House LLC, New York.

WATERBROOK® and its deer colophon are registered trademarks of Penguin Random House LLC.

Library of Congress Cataloging-in-Publication Data
Names: Thompson, Becky (Rebecca F.) author.
Title: Truth unchanging : encountering God in the midst of motherhood / Becky Thompson. Description: First edition. | Colorado Springs, CO : WaterBrook, 2019.
Identifiers: LCCN 2018020841 | ISBN 9780525652298 (hardcover) | ISBN 9780525652472 (ebook)
Subjects: LCSH: Mothers—Religious life. | Mothers—Prayers and devotions.
Classification: LCC BV4529.18 .T467 2019 | DDC 248.8/431—dc23
LC record available at https://lccn.loc.gov/2018020841

Printed in the United States of America
2019—First Edition

10 9 8 7 6 5 4 3 2 1

SPECIAL SALES
Most WaterBrook books are available at special quantity discounts when purchased in bulk by corporations, organizations, and special-interest groups. Custom imprinting or excerpting can also be done to fit special needs. For information, please e-mail specialmarketscms@penguinrandomhouse.com or call 1-800-603-7051.

*For my parents, Marc and Susan Pitts,
who taught me how to hear the voice of Truth
and trust Him no matter where He leads.*

Contents

Contents

To You, Momma, Before We Begin

*W*henever mom friends of mine find the time to read a book, I want to celebrate with them. So let's start there. Look at you! You're making time to do something for yourself. I hope the room is quiet and you're alone, but the reality is your kids might be climbing all over you as you read this. Who knows, maybe you dropped this book onto your passenger seat and you're reading in the school pickup line. Maybe your kids are napping or we're starting the day together before your family wakes up. Or maybe, just maybe, it's the end of the day and you have been looking forward to this alone time since about 9:00 a.m.

I don't know what your moment looks like right now, but I am sure of two things: God is with you as you read, and He desires to speak to you in the pages ahead.

So before we go on, we need to do this very important thing together. Okay? Take a deep breath, and then listen. Take in the sounds of your surroundings. Listen to your home. Listen to the room. Listen to the cars outside, the kids playing, the sounds coming from the baby monitor, the TV, the washing machine running in the background. Whatever noise is around you, just listen to it. I'll wait.

Motherhood is often noisy. It might not be insanely noisy all the time, but as moms our lives are rarely silent.

As a matter of fact, unless everyone is asleep, silence is how we usually know that our children are up to no good. When you're a mom, silence isn't golden. It's suspicious.

But in this moment, I don't want you to just focus on the noise around you. We often try to tune it out anyway. I want you to pay careful attention to the noise within you. That noise often goes unaddressed, but the silent roar of our own thoughts can be overwhelming. It's a mental din of to-do lists and anxieties and possible outcomes for every situation we're facing. We're making notes of what we need to buy or whom we need to contact or what bill we need to pay. We're wondering if our children are on track developmentally, if they're okay, and if they're becoming good people. We are thinking about marriage and money and mothering. We're wondering how to do better in just about every area of our lives.

Our thoughts within us can be just as loud as the noise around us, but they are often harder to silence. So before we continue, I want you to take another deep breath. We are going to quiet our thoughts.

Let's focus our hearts and minds on what God might be speaking to us right now. Let's silence the space within us to make room for the voice of the Lord. Let's pray this simple prayer together.

Mind, focus. Anxieties, go. Heart, open. Lord, come. We desire to meet with You, God. In Jesus's name we come before You. Amen.

Here is some good news before we begin. God wants to speak to His people. Throughout Scripture, God has proven His desire to speak to those He loves. That includes us!

In the beginning, God spoke and formed the world. He spoke to the first man and woman He had created in His image. He taught and led them, and they followed His instructions. Later, when they were separated from Him, His voice pointed to His rescue plan for humanity through the prophets.

God spoke to us through His Son, Jesus, when He came as the Redeemer, making a way for us to have a personal relationship with the Father again. Now the Lord speaks to us through His completed Word and His Holy Spirit, who lives within us, guiding us throughout our lives.

Through God's written Word we learn to recognize the voice of the Lord and the character and nature of our heavenly Father. As we spend time reading, the Holy Spirit reveals the meaning and application of God's Truth, found in Scripture, in our lives. But an incredible thing takes place when we spend time listening to the Holy Spirit as we read God's Word. Our hearts begin to identify God's voice speaking to us in our daily lives.

Just before Jesus went to the cross, He told His friends in John 16:12–14, "I have much more to say to you, more than you can now bear. But when he, the Spirit of truth, comes, he will guide you into all the truth. He will not speak on his own; he will speak only what he hears, and he will tell you what is yet to come. He will glorify me because it is from me that he will receive what he will make known to you."

This Holy Spirit is the one who continues to lead us throughout our daily lives, revealing to us the heart and direction of the Father. His voice doesn't always come audibly. Sometimes, we have a feeling. Sometimes, God speaks to us through a trusted friend, who calls to remind us that we are loved at the moment we needed to hear it most. Sometimes we just know what to do next. But so many of us don't think of these promptings as the voice of the Holy Spirit speaking to us. So we become fooled into thinking that God speaks to everyone but us. We get tricked by our Enemy into believing that we don't personally know the voice of our Lord. But that couldn't be farther from the Truth.

So as moms, how can we tune our hearts to God's voice when our surroundings and our own thoughts can be so noisy? How do we maintain communication with our invisible God when the rush of life means that it's not always possible to have conversations with the people we can see right in front of us? And how can we be certain that what we hear or feel is even the voice of the Lord leading us?

In the pages ahead, we will answer these questions and more. We will go back to the very beginning of Scripture and walk our way through the Word to look at specific moments when God spoke to His people and then listen for what God is saying to us in each story. As we read the words that God has spoken to His people in the past, we will become increasingly familiar with His voice of Truth that continues to speak into our lives today.

I know your life might be in a constant state of change and growth. I know you might feel you are always on the move, keeping up with growing kids and busy schedules, rushing and going and never stopping to rest. But I also know that you desire to be led by God and that's why you're reading these words right now. So, as we spend just a few minutes together each day listening for the voice of God in our lives, I believe that the Lord will meet with us. And we will celebrate that He has been with us all along, leading us by His Holy Spirit and His unchanging Truth.

Becky

I Love Talking to You

God Speaks to Adam and Eve in the Garden

Genesis 1

There is a famous picture of Jesus that hangs in just about every small church in Oklahoma. I bet you have seen it too. It's a portrait of Jesus with soft light-brown hair and a trimmed beard, looking up toward heaven. This guy looks quiet. He looks like the type of man who would walk into a room and sit silently, not speaking but just taking it all in. You know—pensive Jesus.

The thing is, whether or not we've ever seen that particular picture of Jesus hanging on the wall, many of us picture Jesus with the same quiet demeanor in our hearts. Many of us have been taught to remember that He is always in the room with us, but we don't usually imagine Him walking around talking to us in that room.

What if He is? What if we've forgotten that Jesus was a storyteller who loved to sit around the fire and talk with His friends. What if instead of imagining Him looking upward toward the heavens with perfectly combed hair, we imagined a friend standing in our kitchen while we washed dishes or sitting in the passenger seat while we ran errands? What if instead of calling our best friends or our moms or our mentors, we started a conversation with Jesus in the middle of the day? While it might sound strange, that's the type of relationship that God intended for us to have when He originally created us.

Let's go back to the Garden of Eden. God spoke the world into existence. He created everything with His voice, by the power of His word. And then, Scripture says, God had a conversation with Himself. I imagine the Father, Son, and Holy Spirit standing in heaven saying these recorded words: "Let us make mankind in our image, in our likeness."[1] So He did.

God made man and woman and then placed them in a perfect garden and said to them, "Be fruitful and increase in number; fill the earth and subdue it. Rule over the fish in the sea and the birds in the sky and over every living creature that moves on the ground."[2]

Look at what we just read. God designed humanity with the ability to hear His voice and respond to His commands. God created us to be in communication with Him.

So my question is this: Why would we ever dare to believe that the same God who spoke the world into existence, who says in His Word that He "is the same yesterday and today and forever,"[3] suddenly decided to stop talking? We often imagine a conversation with the Lord being very one sided. We speak. He listens. Occasionally, He answers. But the truth is, God started His conversation with His creation in the garden, and our hearts still crave this type of relationship with Him today.

The good news for us is that God is still speaking, and as we listen, I believe He is always reminding our hearts, *"My sheep hear My voice, and I know them."*[4] *I know you. I made you and I love you. I want to lead you, love you, and let you in on the secrets of My heart. This conversation was My idea. You were designed to be in communication with Me. My Word is alive and active.*

It is living. Read My Word anytime You want to hear My voice, but as you do, listen closely. Because I reveal throughout My Word that I speak to the hearts of My people in many different ways. Let's talk. I'm free anytime you are.[5]

What kind of relationship would we have with the Lord if we started to have conversations with the living God? What would our mothering look like if we remembered that we had unlimited access to a parent's greatest resource? God is ready to reveal His Truth; we just need to tune our hearts to His voice.

Lord, thank You for being the God who desires to talk to us. We value Your written Word. Through Your Word, we know what You say and what You sound like when You speak to us. Help us hear Your voice speaking to us throughout the day. Change the images we have of You in our hearts if they are not accurate representations of who You really are. Help us get to know You so personally, God. Give us ears to hear Your Truth. In Jesus's name we pray. Amen.

You Heard Me

God Gives the First Instructions

Genesis 3

---

*I*t was a beautiful morning in southern California. We had been living in our new rental house for about six weeks, and I decided that I would take my youngest two out to find the local library while my oldest was in school.

On our way out the door, I thought, *I need to run a load of towels through the washing machine. I'll just throw those in, and they'll be ready to dry when we get home in an hour or so.*

But as I walked into the laundry room, I had this unusual thought: *I shouldn't run the washing machine while I'm away from the house.*

It was so strange because I've left the house while the washing machine was running hundreds of times in my life. *Nah. It's fine. What could happen?* I thought. I grabbed the towels from the basket and threw them in, then added some detergent and started the cycle.

I had no idea that the hose that connects the washing machine to the drain would come loose and pour gallons of water all over the house. Or that water would flood into the kitchen and the garage and the hallway into the bedroom. Or that it would soak the carpet and cause such a huge mess. But God knew.

Here's the thing. When God speaks to us, it doesn't always make sense from our perspective. We might even ignore it. But this place of uncertainty is where the Enemy sneaks in.

The first attack on the hearts of humanity was an attack against the voice of the Lord and our ability to hear and understand Him correctly.

After God made the garden and placed Adam and Eve in it, He gave them specific instructions. He told them they could eat from any tree except the tree of the knowledge of good and evil. God said, "Don't eat this fruit because then you will know both good and evil. You will become like God, and then you will know what it means to be unlike God." So, very simple directions. Hard to miss if you ask me.

But one day, Adam and Eve walked a little too close to that particular tree. Scripture says that the snake (our Enemy) was crafty, and from the tree he asked Eve, "Did God really say, 'You must not eat from any tree in the garden'?"[6]

Eve knew the answer. She replied, "We may eat fruit from the trees in the garden, but God did say, 'You must not eat fruit from the tree that is in the middle of the garden, and you must not touch it, or you will die.'"[7]

But the snake went on to cause her to doubt. He made her question.

And do you know, he tries to get us to fall for the same thing Eve did. It is his oldest tactic to pull our hearts away from Truth by asking us, "Did God really say? Did you really hear God say that? Are you sure? Do you really hear the voice of the Lord?" And we begin to wonder . . . *Did He?*

The promptings of God in our life, like *"Don't run the washing machine when you're away,"* or *"Encourage that other mom in the store,"* or *"Throw an extra change of clothes into the diaper bag"* don't come with the same kind of consequence that Adam and Eve experienced when they ate the forbidden fruit. But they are still important to follow.

Each instruction that God gives us is calling us down the best path to our future. It's not uncommon for God's people to wonder if those little nudges are really from the Lord, but the beautiful truth is, the more we respond to these promptings, even when we don't understand them, the more we will train our hearts to listen for God's loving direction in all situations.

Today, I believe the Lord is reminding us, *I told you what to do because I love you. Trust that you hear Me. You know My voice. Lean into the leading. When the Enemy would try to create doubt or confusion, cling to My Truth. It might not make sense, but I have a purpose.*

Lord, we were created to trust You. Like Eve, we were designed to know You and Your voice. I pray that we would not fall victim to the same lies that fooled Eve. Help us stay rooted in Truth. In Jesus's name we pray. Amen.

Who Told You That You Needed to Hide?

God Calls to Adam and Eve in the Garden

Genesis 3

He was sitting behind the couch, doing his best not to be found, and he was doing a good job of it. I knew my youngest son, Jaxton, who was three at the time, had been playing in the craft supplies. He knew which ones he was allowed to touch and which ones he was supposed to leave alone. As I cleaned the house and made my way past him a few times, I saw that he was using the crayons and stickers mostly. But when I came back through the living room with a load of laundry and he wasn't where he had been, I called out to him.

No answer.

I looked for him in all the usual places, and I started to get a little worried when he wasn't in any of them. I called louder, "Jaxton! Jax! Buddy! You're not in trouble! Where are you?" That's when I noticed that the couch was pushed slightly forward from the wall. I leaned over the top and peeked down at him.

"Why are you hiding from Momma?" I asked. I looked around the room for a clue to tell me what might be wrong. Other than the usual mess, nothing seemed out of the ordinary. "Come here. You're not in trouble," I offered as I helped him out from behind the couch and onto my lap. "Did you play with something you shouldn't have?"

He nodded.

"Can you show me?"

He led me to a bottle of purple paint and to a place on a nearby basket that had the slightest purple hue to it that definitely wasn't there before.

"Did you use the paints Momma told you not to touch?"

He snuggled deeper into me.

We had a short talk about why there are some things that I don't want him to touch, and then I reminded him that the best thing to do when he has done something wrong is come to me so I can help him fix it. "You don't need to hide," I comforted.

As he ran off to play, I thought of all the times I have felt like hiding because I have done something wrong. This reaction is just about as old as time itself.

The Word says that in the garden, after Adam and Eve were deceived by the snake, they fashioned clothing for themselves from leaves and hid among the trees. Can you imagine the two of them, wearing leaves, ducking behind a bush, believing they could hide from God?

But wait. Do *we* ever think we can hide from Him too? Do we ever allow shame to tell us that we should avoid bringing our mistakes to the Lord and just avoid addressing them in His presence?

The truth is, when Adam and Eve hid, God sought them out, asking, "Where are you?"[8] He didn't leave them in their shame.

This is what He calls out to our hearts again and again. Just as I called my little boy out of his guilt, God is constantly calling to us. When shame says, *"You made a mistake and God will be upset with you,"* the Lord says, *Who told* you that you had a reason to hide? What are you doing behind that tree? That busyness? That distraction? Why are you keeping yourself from My presence? Come out from everything that would keep you away from Me. There's no condemnation. When you feel like you've fallen short, come closer to Me. I am full of mercy.* And as we retrain our ears to listen for His voice of Truth, we will be able to easily recognize the difference between the voice of guilt and the voice of grace.

Lord, thank You for allowing us to come before Your throne when we feel like we least deserve it. Guilt wants to keep us separated from You, but we know that when we make a mistake or fall short, Your love is waiting to welcome our repentant hearts. We hear You inviting us out from hiding, and we make the choice to allow ourselves to be held by the arms of grace. In Jesus's name we pray. Amen.

Don't Misunderstand My Love

God Tells Adam and Eve to Leave the Garden

Genesis 3

We moved to California in December of 2017 after thirty years of living in Oklahoma. There are plenty of ways that California is different from Oklahoma, but there are a few laws I'm still getting used to. For example, you're not supposed to hold your cell phone even while stopped at a stoplight. I get it. Traffic here is nuts and lawmakers are just trying to keep people safe. But this means that I usually ask Siri to text for me.

Siri doesn't always listen well. Sometimes Siri just gets it wrong. I mean, once I just wanted to text a friend that I was grateful for the love of Jesus, and Siri heard me say that I was grateful for the olives and cheese sauce. Siri heard, but she didn't understand.

And Lord forgive me, but sometimes I'm just like her. Sometimes I hear but don't understand.

There are times I believe that God is trying to tell me something and I'm filtering His words through my own feelings or personal motives. We often do this with stories we have read in Scripture.

Do you have one of those beginner's Bibles with the colorful pictures?

Maybe it was yours or maybe you have one for your kids. The saddest page of Adam and Eve's story shows them holding each other and leaving the garden with their little fig-leaf clothes and their sorrowful faces. When we were young, many of us were taught that because Adam and Eve disobeyed, they were punished and had to leave this paradise God had made for them.

This conclusion is mostly true, but we miss that this story is actually a beautiful picture of God's mercy. Adam and Eve did disobey God. They did do something God told them not to, and in that moment they stopped being perfect reflections of the Lord. They couldn't remain in the presence of a perfectly Holy God as they had before. They had to be separated.

But God didn't want them to stay in this state of separation from His original design forever. He created them to walk and talk with Him. He wanted this relationship restored, but restoration was in danger if Adam and Eve stayed in the garden.

Remember that when God made the garden, there were many trees, but two trees were mentioned by name—the tree of the knowledge of good and evil and the tree of life. God had warned that they could not eat from the tree of the knowledge of good and evil, but what was so significant about the second tree?

When Adam and Eve sinned, God said, "The man has now become like one of us, knowing good and evil. He must not be allowed to reach out his hand and take also from the tree of life and eat, and live forever."[9]

If they had eaten from this tree, Adam and Eve would have lived forever in a state of eternal separation from God. And God loved them too much to allow this to happen. He kept them from the tree of life so He could send His Son to restore humanity to right relationship with Himself.

When we read that God said Adam and Eve had to go, many of us hear punishment. We hear banishment. But God was saying so much more. He was saying, *"I love them too much to be separated from them forever."*

I think we all have places in our lives where we need to reevaluate what God has said to us. Perhaps we have always heard God's words through a filter of judgment, when we need to filter everything we hear God say through the filter of His love. We need to hear His words and His heart. Today, I believe the Lord would say to us, *I loved you too much. That's why I did it. I loved you too much, and that's why I kept you from it. I loved you too much. That's why I answered you the way I did. It wasn't to punish. It wasn't to hurt. It wasn't because I am cruel. Everything that I have ever done for you is compelled by My love. Hear My heart today. I am good.*

Lord, today we choose to repent for the moments we misunderstood You, and we thank You for being the God who redeems. We want to hear Your Word and understand Your heart. In Jesus's name we pray. Amen.

Wait. It's a Redemption Story

God Speaks to Noah

Genesis 6–9

Maybe someday, I'll tell the story about the hardest two years of my life. The story about how I didn't know if my marriage would make it. The story of hurt and betrayal. The story I'm not sure I want my children to read in a book when they're grown. But until then, I'll share this. My husband and I have been in seasons when according to the world's standards, the smartest decision would have been to just walk away. When divorce looked like the healthiest option for both of us if we wanted to move forward with whole and complete hearts.

At least, that's how it looked. The truth is, that season wasn't the full story. Because while it appeared from all angles like the story of loss and heartache, God was writing the story of grace and forgiveness. God was writing a redemption story.

Have you experienced a season like this in your own life? Have you been in a season when everything looked like it was over? Where life seemed as though it would never go back to what it was before? When you were just sure that God was busy with something else and that ache of sadness or desperation or discouragement would never leave? Maybe it wasn't a relationship. Maybe it was a career

13

or a city you had to leave. Maybe it was a project or a dream that ended suddenly. Oh, friend, perhaps it was a loss of someone you loved dearly. Maybe you're living this story even now.

What do we do when our whole lives seem consumed by loss? What is God saying then? Where is the voice of the Lord in the midst of that kind of heartache? Where is God when we feel lost in a sea of sadness? I wonder if Noah ever asked this question.

When we think of the story of Noah, we often focus on the rainbow and the animals. We look at what God saved. We focus on the promise at the end, but from the middle of the story, I bet it felt pretty hopeless. I bet the moment the waters began to rise and the skies began to open, Noah looked out across all the loss and devastation and felt overwhelmed. Do you suppose?

Do you think that at any time during the nearly four hundred days Noah spent on the ark he felt discouraged? That's a long time to be the sole survivors of the planet, stuck on a boat with a ton of animals and no land in sight. I wonder if Noah ever questioned God. I wonder if he was ever afraid. I wonder if the whole thing felt more like an abandonment than a rescue.

The heart of this story isn't that God destroyed all life on earth. The beauty of the flood is that while God could have just started over, He chose to preserve life through Noah. He continued the redemption story of sinful man through Noah's obedience and a boat until God could send Jesus to a cross to save us once and for all. Noah might not have been able to see the big picture from the middle of it, but the flood wasn't the story of destruction. It was the story of God's preservation.[10]

You know, in the middle of the craziness that is our lives, sometimes we feel as if it's all chaos. We feel it's just completely hopeless, the waters are never going to recede, and we're just floating in the middle of an endless ocean of confusion.

But just when things seem to be at their worst, the Lord whispers to us, *It's a redemption story. It's a story of My mercy. It's not over. It's a story where life will be saved through My goodness alone. Don't get stuck in the middle and believe it's the end. You will reach dry land, and you will see that I keep My promises and have been with You from rain to rainbow.*

The voice that told Noah to go into the ark was the same voice that called him out. His voice is still trustworthy in all seasons.

Lord, help us hear Your voice even when all hope seems lost. God, You are our refuge when the waters rise. You are our shelter when the skies pour. We put all our hope in You and trust that you are writing a redemption story for each of us. In Jesus's name we pray. Amen.

There Are People Waiting on Your Obedience

God Speaks to Abraham

Genesis 12

One of my favorite moments of motherhood took place in a small café. I had two small children at the time, and I was a stay-at-home mom. I didn't have many mom friends, and other than keeping the kids alive and the house in reasonable order, I was kind of bored. Only moms understand this feeling. Exhausted, overworked, spread thin . . . and yet bored with the same cycle of to-dos every day.

During this season, I would use lunchtime as an opportunity to get out of the house and connect with other adults even if they were strangers at a restaurant. While we were out for lunch this particular afternoon, my son decided that he wanted to know if a stranger in the café had met Jesus yet. He began to ask loudly, "MOM! MOM! Does that man know Jesus?" This wasn't the type of interaction I was hoping for. I just wanted a sandwich and to be around other people. I didn't want to have to preach the gospel.

I nervously told my son that I didn't know that man or if he knew Jesus, and then we took our lunch to go. All the way home I felt God tugging at my heart;

I should have stayed and spoken to that man. When we arrived home, it was clear. The Lord was asking me to go back.

Nervously, we returned to the café, and after a short conversation with the man, I understood exactly why God had put this on my heart. That small moment of obedience impacted the man in the café. It impacted my children, and I think I was the most impacted by those few minutes.

Since that moment, I've learned that when God asks us to go out of our way, even into uncomfortable situations, our obedience isn't just for our benefit. It is always for the benefit of others as well. There are always people waiting on the other side of our obedience.

In Scripture we find an example of what obedience meant in the life of Abraham. One of Noah's descendants, Abraham (then called Abram), was called by God to be set apart from everyone else on the earth. God said, "Go from your country, your people and your father's household to the land I will show you. I will make you into a great nation, and I will bless you; I will make your name great . . . and all peoples on earth will be blessed through you."[11]

We know God kept His word, because God promised to bless all people on earth through Abraham, and Jesus was one of Abraham's descendants. Jesus was part of God's promise to Abraham. But it all hinged on Abraham's obedience to do what God had said. "Go from your country to the land I will show you." First the obedience. Then the blessing.

In our own lives, it can be so hard to understand why God calls us to certain things. Why He wants us to make that phone call or enroll our child in that school. Why He says things like *Talk to that mom* or *Offer to host that event.*

But the truth is, God intends to bless us and bless others through these opportunities that He gives us to be obedient. Today I believe He's reminding both of us that our obedience has never just been for our own good. It has always been for the good of others as well. I believe He's reminding us today, *Make yourself available to be used by Me today, and together we can impact hearts. You are My ambassador on the earth, and My invitation for you to reach out to others has never been just for your benefit. I want to show you how much your life matters to the world around you. You were created to carry My light into the darkness. You were created to be a conduit of My blessings. I'm not calling you to make you uncomfortable. I'm calling you to action so I can bless your obedience.*

Our children, our families, our friends, and our communities are all waiting for us to decide if we are going to listen to the Lord's promptings. How willing will we be to go out of our way to do what He says?

Lord, help us not become so busy that we miss Your voice calling us to share Your love with the world around us. Teach us how to respond in obedience, remembering that there are people waiting for us to say yes to You. In Jesus's name we pray. Amen.

Trust the Path

God Calls Lot to the Mountains

Genesis 19

I just don't think I can do it, God." I've said this more than once in my life. I said it just days before I was supposed to give birth (to each of my children). I've said it when God called me to start new ventures. I said it daily as our big move across the country got closer. And yet, the Lord accomplished everything that He began in me. It didn't matter whether or not I thought I could do it. What matters is His continual faithfulness. God doesn't call us to anything that He doesn't have full provision to accomplish in our lives.

He doesn't first say, "Do this," and then work on a plan as He figures out how it will happen. No, God calls us to take on assignments that He already has a plan to complete. But I've done my fair share of arguing with Him. I've done my best to try to convince Him that I know better than He does. I bet I'm the only one who does this. I bet you've never argued with the Lord. *wink wink*

Lot, Abraham's nephew, argued with an angel who brought a message from the Lord. Lot and his family were living in Sodom just before God intended to destroy it. Because of the promise God had made to Abraham, God sent angels to rescue Lot and his family, to get them out of this city before destruction came. As morning approached, angels took Lot and his family by the hands and led them out of the city, saying, "Flee for your lives! Don't look back, and don't stop anywhere in the plain! Flee to the mountains or you will be swept away!"[12]

I know how I would have responded in this situation. I would have run! But Lot's response?

"No, my lords, please! Your servant has found favor in your eyes, and you have shown great kindness to me in sparing my life. But I can't flee to the mountains; this disaster will overtake me, and I'll die. Look, here is a town near enough to run to, and it is small. Let me flee to it—it is very small, isn't it? Then my life will be spared."[13]

Lot said, "Look! There's a little town! I can't make it to the mountains, but I can make it over there." The angel agreed, and Lot and his family (except for his wife who made the mistake of looking back) found refuge without having to go all the way up the mountain.

It would be easy to read this and think that Lot changed God's plan. It would be easy to think that because Lot was not certain he could make it to the mountains, God allowed him to go just to the nearby town instead.

But we read in the next few verses that Lot and his family went on to live in the mountains. They eventually made it to the place God was calling them.

Lot didn't change God's plan for his life. He just added a stop and shifted the timeline a little.

My question for you is, What is God calling you to today that you are trying to compromise about? What are you trying to argue yourself out of doing? Where are you trying to convince God that you don't really need to go?

Because there is no safer place than the perfect will of God for you. There's no place better for you to be than exactly where He calls. And to each of us today, I believe He is saying, *Look up to the mountains. I'm calling you higher up and farther up into My presence! Dream bigger. Aim higher. Believe deeper. You are going to make it. And the sooner you trust Me, the sooner you will get to where I'm calling your heart.*

I wonder what greatness waits for you in the perfect plan of God? It's probably not nearly as overwhelming as it appears on this side of the climb.

Lord, You are faithful, and You have full provision to help us accomplish everything You have set before us. When we don't think we can make it, remind our hearts that You are calling us to take on certain mountains for a reason. In Jesus's name we pray. Amen.

My Way Is Best

God Promises Sarah a Child

Genesis 15–21

I had decided to build a bench for our entryway because Pinterest had convinced me that I really needed one. With two small children at the time, I somehow managed to have the legs, upholstered seat, and stain all completed during naptime. When my husband walked in the door and I said, "Would you like to sit here and take off your boots?" I think he was surprised, but in eight years of marriage, my husband had already learned that I like to prove to others that I can take care of hard things by myself without any help. Do you ever feel this way too?

I think, *I can do it by myself. I've got this. I'm amazing. I'm capable.* And while this sort of self-determination and self-confidence is important, let me be clear that in my life I have had to learn the hard way a few times that Jesus did not create me to take care of everything on my own without any of *His* input or help. I have had to learn that He actually has some pretty insightful advice on how to accomplish just about everything, and He offers it willingly if I don't get ahead of myself and try to do it on my own without Him.

Sarah, Abraham's wife, learned this lesson the hard way. After God promised to bless Abraham's descendants, Sarah (then called Sarai) questioned how this could be possible since she was unable to have children. She had been barren, and she was old. In her heart, she believed the promise of God was true, but she just couldn't see *how* He was going to fulfill it. So Sarah did what made the most sense to her. She tried to figure it out on her own. Sarah offered her maidservant to Abraham and said that Abraham could have a child with this woman as a way to accomplish God's promise.

The only problem was, this wasn't God's original plan. Abraham did have a child by the maidservant, Hagar. But Sarah didn't know that God would give her a child in her old age too and this child, Isaac, would be the heir God had intended.[14]

Sometimes we are just like Sarah. We make decisions that seem the most sensible to us. We take projects out of God's hands and timing and into our own hands. We set out to accomplish what God has told us to do using what we see in front of us as the means to decide what to do next. When really our marriages, our parenting, our work, our ministries, our friends . . . all of it . . . fall into the category of things God takes care of well. We just have to be patient and follow His process.

We have to remember that when we think, *I've got it. I'll figure it out on my own,* God says, *"I know what I'm doing. I know that there are answers that don't seem to be coming yet, but I want you to stay with Me and not get ahead of yourself. Don't try to do this on your own. Don't take this out of My hands. Allow Me to be in charge of this process. I know how this works out. Rely on My wisdom. Trust My heart. Wait for Me to show you what to do next, even if the timing doesn't make sense to you and even if you can't see how I'm going to do it. I have good plans for you."*

Placing what we care about most in the hands of the Lord can be so difficult.

Choosing not to go forward until the Lord reveals the next step can feel equally impossible when we just want to do it all on our own. But allowing the Lord to complete His promise in His timing without trying to change it is a sign of spiritual maturity. God is helping us become women who are strong enough to carry the weight of patience.

Lord, forgive us for the times we thought we knew better than You did. Forgive us for the times we said we could do it on our own. We don't want to have to backtrack, God. We don't want to get so far down the line of our own strategy that we have to come back and say, "Let's try it Your way this time." Help us live as if we believe You know what You're doing. In Jesus's name we pray. Amen.

I See You Right Where You Are

God Speaks to Hagar

Genesis 16

There are some women who have beautifully decorated office spaces. Carefully chosen photos and organized desks are the background of their work lives. While I now have a desk to call my own here in California, when we lived in Oklahoma, I worked out of my cloffice. (That's a walk-in closet that I used as an office for about seven years, if you were wondering.) Leaning up against the back wall of my closet with my laptop on my knees and my husband's shirts to my side, I'd think and write free of distractions.

Why work from this space? Well, I was working from home with three kids in the house; the two locked doors between that closet and the rest of the house helped my husband keep the kids from "finding me." I had some life-changing phone calls from that closet. I also had some really important conversations with the Lord in that space.

One afternoon, my husband had come home early from work, and I needed a break. You know how there are times when you *want* a break and other times when you *need* a break? That's where I was. My heart was overwhelmed with a family crisis, and I just needed a minute to be alone. I needed to cry. I needed to let myself completely fall apart without having to also think about getting a toy bucket out for a kid, or breaking up an argument, or fixing a snack for someone.

I went into my closet/office, slid down onto the floor . . . and just cried.

I felt absolutely alone. I felt tucked into a space where no one really knew how deeply my heart ached. I remember crying out, "Do You even see me, God? Do you have a plan for how You will help us get through this? Do You even know what it is going to take to get us to the other side? Because I can't see it. I feel so alone. I feel so completely alone."

I wish that I could tell you that the Lord appeared to me in a glowing vision of holiness and gave me the next few months of strategy. But that didn't happen. Instead, the Lord simply whispered, *I see you.* And that was enough. There is something about being seen as we truly are that starts the inflation of hope. Praise the Lord, we serve the God who sees us—El Roi.

This is one of God's many names revealed to us throughout Scripture, and the woman who declared it first was Hagar, Sarah's servant. After Hagar became pregnant with Abraham's child, she ended up alone in the desert. She had been bragging that she was able to have children when Sarah still couldn't, and full of pain and anger, Sarah began to treat Hagar harshly. Sarah treated Hagar so terribly that Hagar ran for her life. Alone, afraid, and pregnant in the wilderness, Hagar began to cry.

But she wasn't alone for long. Scripture says that God found Hagar and spoke to her. He told her what would come next. He told her what to do, saying, "You are now pregnant and you will give birth to a son. You shall name him Ishmael, for the LORD has heard of your misery."

Hagar responded, "You are the God who sees me, . . . I have now seen the One who sees me."[15]

In her moment of total hopelessness, God saw Hagar and spoke to her need.

And the God who found Hagar in the desert was the same God who spoke to me in my closet. He's the God who sees you right where you are too. He's the God who finds us in our pain and doesn't leave us alone in it. He's the same God who has been with us in every moment of our sorrow and suffering, and He says the same thing to us. *I see you. I see your pain. I see your heartache. I see your confusion. I see how much you need Me, and I'm not going to leave you out here to suffer alone. When you thought no one else knew or understood or saw you, I did. You're not abandoned. We'll do this together. We'll face it together. We'll get through it together.*

There are so many moments of motherhood when it feels as though absolutely no one understands and no one sees us. In those moments especially, God compassionately holds us close and reminds our hearts that we are completely seen, known, and loved.

Lord, thank You for not leaving us alone to face what is heaviest on our hearts. Even though our moments of sorrow are loud, Your love is always louder. Help us continue to hear Your voice reminding us that You are the God who sees. In Jesus's name we pray. Amen.

Do This Until I Tell You What's Next

God Tells Abraham to Sacrifice Isaac

Genesis 22

As parents, my husband and I have made a point to recognize that what might be best for one of our children might not always be best for all of them. This is even true when it comes to schooling. We had always planned to put our children in public school, and while two of my children currently do attend public school, one of my kids is homeschooled. This was not part of my plan. Yet when the Lord spoke to my heart and prompted me to teach this child at home, immediately a peace came over me. Despite the newness and uncertainty that I would face entering this unfamiliar season as a homeschooling mom, I now had a settled confidence that this was the right decision. I wasn't sure how long we'd be schooling at home, but I knew that God had said to do it. So I was prepared to do it until He said to do something else. Secretly, my fingers were crossed that He'd say something else within the year. (He didn't, if you were wondering.)

This is what God does, though. He doesn't change. But sometimes He will add to the instructions He has already provided. This may even leave us wondering if we heard Him correctly in the first place. *Was that really the Lord who instructed me to begin the process if we weren't going to complete it? Was it really the Lord who asked me to take on that assignment if He was going to seem to change His mind?*

When we get started down the path that God has called us, it's important that we do what He's called us to do until He adds to His instructions.

Abraham lived this. His son Isaac, the boy God had promised him, was loved. He was the son through which God would continue His plan for the redemption of the world. But God called to Abraham and asked him to take Isaac up the mountain and offer him as a sacrifice.[16]

Can you imagine? Can you imagine God asking you to give up the precious promise He had given to you?

Abraham was faithful to do exactly as the Lord had commanded. He didn't stop. He didn't waver. He just began the climb with his son. When Isaac asked how they'd be making a sacrifice without a lamb, Abraham confidently replied, "God himself will provide the lamb for the burnt offering, my son."[17]

Even though God had said to take Isaac up the mountain and offer him as a sacrifice, I don't think Abraham ever believed he would have to sacrifice his own son. Yet he was faithful to do just as God had instructed him right up until the moment God cried from heaven, "Do not lay a hand on the boy!" God provided a ram caught in the thicket. This is what Abraham sacrificed to the Lord on the mountain he named "The LORD Will Provide." [18]

These moments (although much less dramatic) occur in our lives as well. God gives us instructions, and sometimes as we are faithfully doing what He has called us to do, He updates the plan. He adds to what He has already told us to do, and we have to shift directions. Have you ever experienced this? A time when you were sure God led you to do something and you faithfully did it, but suddenly it ended or you felt called to do something completely different? Maybe

God told you to start a job and then asked you to leave it just a few months later. Maybe God put it on your heart to begin a project or a ministry in your church and then told you to pass it along to someone else. Maybe He told you to stay at home, only to tell you to go back to work after a year.

While our Enemy would have us believe that God is untrustworthy because things didn't work out the way we believed they would or God seemed to change His mind, we listen to the voice of Truth. God reminds us, *I didn't change My mind. I just revealed the next part of the plan. I see your obedience. I'm asking you to do what I have told you until I tell you to do the next thing. Stay close to Me so that you know exactly where I'm leading you. Listen for My voice to guide you carefully. Each step is calculated. Each is on purpose. Be confident in My loving instruction.*

Lord, we will take the steps right in front of us until we hear You saying stop. We choose not to demand answers for how this will all turn out. Instead, we trust each step as it comes and commit ourselves to each assignment You give us. In Jesus's name we pray. Amen.

I'll Tell You What's Really Going On

God Speaks to Rebekah

Genesis 25

My nine-year-old son, Kolton, is usually levelheaded. He is a kid who is in touch with his emotions, but they don't boss him around. Do you know a kid like this? Kolton might cry. He might fuss. But he decides when and where. One afternoon, he was uncharacteristically upset. He yelled at his sister and was short with all of us. Because I know my son, I knew that this unusual behavior was like a check-engine light for his heart. His emotions were telling me that something else was going on that I couldn't see.

I invited him into a quiet space and asked, "What's really going on, son? What's really bothering you?" We had a good conversation that afternoon. We looked into some of the deeper heart issues he was facing and said a prayer together.

I have realized that moments like these are a gift. When we can notice that there is something going on that is bigger than what we can see and feel, and we can pause to address it, there is so much growth that can take place in those moments. We just have to possess the wisdom to stop and ask, "What's really going on?"

Sometimes my emotions are like my son's. When I feel out of sorts or I feel overwhelmed, when I am short with my kids or I'm stressed or on edge, I need to stop and ask myself, *What's really going on here?* And when I can't be sure, when I don't know exactly what's happening in my heart, I have the ability to go to my Father for His perspective and His reassuring voice to help me figure out what needs to be addressed in my heart.

There is a woman in Scripture who knew to inquire of the Lord when something seemed a little off in her life. In Genesis, we discover that Abraham's son, Isaac, married a woman named Rebekah. She became pregnant with twins and felt them struggling in her womb. Scripture says she went to ask the Lord about it. "Why is this happening to me?" she asked. And the Lord answered, "Two nations are in your womb; and two peoples will be separated from your body; and one people shall be stronger than the other; and the older shall serve the younger."[19]

In essence, God said, "You feel struggling, but here's what's really going on."

What Rebekah felt inside her was the symptom of a deeper issue, and to discover the heart of this issue, she just had to ask, "What's really going on, God? Why is this happening to me?"

As moms, we get to help our children discover what's going on in their hearts. We get to provide our outside perspective and help them navigate the areas of their wills and emotions that seem too big for them to process alone. The beautiful truth is that God does the same thing for us. Just as He shared with Rebekah the bigger picture of what was taking place within her, He wants to share with us His perspective on what's going on within us. He wants to answer our question, *Why is this happening to me?*

While we might not be able to identify it, while we might not see the root of our stress or our heartache or our questioning, God knows, and He says, *Let's talk about it. Let Me share with You the bigger picture here. Let Me gently reveal why you feel the way you do. Let Me tell you what I see. Let Me show you what I know. I see where this all began and what it will become. So let Me help you address it now. Let My love help you reset your heart.*

God has been our Father for a very long time. He knows us better than anyone. And just as we can tell when our kids are off or struggling, God knows when there's more going on with us, and He doesn't leave us in it. He sees what's really going on and helps us address it when we bring our hearts before Him.

Lord, thank You for being a Dad who wants to help us address the root of our symptoms. You don't just point them out God; You bring Your power and Your love, and You right every wrong within us. Remind us to come to You whenever we feel unsettled, confident that You are the answer we need. In Jesus's name we pray. Amen.

Remember, I Am with You

God Speaks to Jacob

Genesis 28

A few weeks ago, I went to the park with my kids. Park time for me now isn't what it was a few years ago when they were smaller. The park used to mean pushing swings, helping them across monkey bars, and making sure no one climbed too high or threw sand.

Now that my kids are older, I spend most of my time supervising and making sure that my youngest, who is still three years old, doesn't try to follow his older brother and sister onto a part of the play equipment that is too big for him. So that afternoon when I saw my daughter going up a faux rock wall, I knew it wouldn't be long before her little brother would follow behind her. As he started to go up, I stood up from the nearby bench where I was watching and began walking over to my little guy. He didn't see me coming. He was too focused on the task in front of him. So when he turned his head to shout "Mooo . . . ," his voice trailed off. He saw that I was already behind him, waiting with my arms out. He laughed, saying, "I didn't knowd you were back dere." I helped him down, and he ran off to take on his next challenge.

When I think of that afternoon, I think about how Jesus is just like that. Before we are even aware of His presence, Jesus has already stepped into the perfect position in our lives. In the Bible, Jacob—one of the twins who were struggling in Rebekah's womb—had a moment similar to my son's. In Genesis, the story of Rebekah's sons continues to unfold. The Lord had said to her that the two children would be like two nations and the older brother would serve the younger brother. This came to pass after the younger brother, Jacob, stole the inheritance and blessing from the older brother, Esau.

As you can imagine, Esau wasn't too happy about it and sought to kill his brother. When Jacob heard this, he left home. It was on his journey that Jacob encountered the Lord.

After traveling all day, Jacob stopped for the night, and that night he had a remarkable dream. In his dream, he saw a staircase with angels ascending and descending and, at the top of the staircase, the Lord stood speaking to him.

" 'I am the LORD, the God of your father Abraham and the God of Isaac. I will give you and your descendants the land on which you are lying. . . . All peoples on earth will be blessed through you and your offspring. I am with you and will watch over you wherever you go.' When Jacob awoke from his sleep, he thought, 'Surely the LORD is in this place, and I was not aware of it!' "[20]

Jacob didn't just encounter the Lord. He had a revelation of understanding that he had been in the presence of the Lord and didn't even realize it.

I think that's you and me too. I know that I rush right by what God tries to reveal to me. I know that when my kids snuggle into me and I experience their love, it's a moment that God has gifted me. I know that when I get to care for them in the most basic ways, it's an opportunity to love them the way Jesus does. I know that when I calm fears and I break up fights and teach young hearts how to be obedient, what I'm doing is far more spectacular than it feels most days. It's holy work. It's an opportunity to meet with God as He guides me in what to say and do.

In all our rushing, in all our ordinary, in all the regular stuff that makes up our story, we are like Jacob, who goes to sleep at the end of the day and says, "God was here all along!? God was with me?!"

Sometimes it just takes a reminder for our spiritual eyes to see exactly where God was and where He is.

Today, I believe He's saying, *I've been here all along. I was in this place, and you didn't even know it. I was with you, and you didn't see. I know that there are places where you questioned My presence. I know that there are some moments that are hard to revisit. But I have been with you through it all. I'm in the ordinary. I'm in the wilderness. I'm in your coming and your going. I have never left you. Remember, I am with you and will watch over you wherever you go.*

Lord, open our eyes to see the places where You have been. Open our hearts to receive the Truth that You promise to go forward with us from this point. We don't want to go through our day unaware of Your presence in our lives. We know we need Your love to help us make it through all we'll face up ahead. Forgive us for the moments we were unaware, and help us remember always that You will never leave us. In Jesus's name we pray. Amen.

I'm Your God

God Calls Jacob Back to Bethel

Genesis 35

I found out that I was pregnant with my second baby when my oldest, Kolton, wasn't even ten months old. In addition to the predictable fears as I tried to figure out how I would hold two babies in my arms and keep up with two very young children, I was also afraid that my love would run out. I remember rocking Kolton to sleep one night thinking, *How am I going to love anyone as much as I love you? How will it be possible to give away more love to anyone else? I love you completely.* It really concerned me that a new baby would steal my love away from him. How could I possibly divide my affection between two children?

When my daughter, Kadence, was born, I discovered what every mom or dad of multiple children learns quickly. Parents love each of their children with their whole hearts.

I wonder if we ever feel like God doesn't love us as much as He loves everyone else. I wonder if, although we have been told that He does, we ever doubt, thinking perhaps He really likes a few other people a little bit more. If we can love our children with our whole hearts, and we are imperfect, why would we believe the lie that God loves us just a little bit less? God loves His children perfectly.

Yet Jesus said something recorded in John 17 about His Father's love that is still sometimes hard for me to understand. While praying to the Father, Jesus said, "The world will know that you sent me and have loved them even as you have loved me."[21] It's one thing to say that God loves each of us with His whole heart, but to say that He loves each of us as much as He loves Jesus? That changes things. Doesn't it? In light of that verse alone, God's love for us seems powerfully personal.

Jacob, Rebekah's son, discovered the intimate love of God in the desert when he was fleeing from his brother, Esau. But this wasn't the only time God appeared to Jacob. One of the most personal encounters Jacob had with the Lord can be found in Genesis 35.

After many years, God called Jacob back to Bethel, the place where Jacob first encountered Him. When Jacob arrived, God came before him and said, "I am God Almighty; be fruitful and increase in number. A nation and a community of nations will come from you, and kings will be among your descendants. The land I gave to Abraham and Isaac I also give to you, and I will give this land to your descendants after you."[22]

Something very personal was happening here between Jacob and the Lord. God had been with him. God had been for him. But in this place, God became fully his.

This is where God extended to Jacob the same blessings that He had given to his father and grandfather. This is where God said, "Now I give the land to you and to all your people who will live after you."

When we entered into a relationship with Jesus, we began to understand that Jesus didn't just die for everyone else. We didn't just come as part of a package deal. He didn't just die for our parents or our grandparents. God loves us, and Jesus died for us. The Truth is, if Jesus could have died and saved only you, the Father would have still sent Him.

Even after the first encounter we have with the Lord, I think our hearts yearn to hear God reminding us again, *I love you personally and completely. I love you fully and uniquely. You're not just one in a crowd; you were the one I was thinking of when I sent Jesus to the cross. I love you as much as I love My Son. My blessings are for you too. My promises are for you too. Rest today in the assurance that My love for you isn't limited.*

Lord, just as we love our children with our whole hearts, You love us with all of Yours. Help us live in a way that shows we believe that. Let that Truth settle over our hearts with peace today. Thank You, God. In Jesus's name we pray. Amen.

Let Me Show You

God Speaks to Joseph Through Dreams

Genesis 37

When it comes to helping my kids with their math homework or helping them practice for a soccer game or helping them figure out a video game, I'm a shower. That's show-er . . . not shower. I'd rather just show them how to do it than explain with plain old words. This works great for two-thirds of my children. My son Kolton doesn't want to be shown. He wants to be told. Turns out, he's just like his daddy.

One afternoon, Kolton was sitting at the kitchen counter, and he needed help with a specific math problem. The first thing I did was ask for his pencil. How was I supposed to just tell him how to do it without showing him? I planned to write out a similar problem and use that problem to show him how he could solve his.

"Here, give me your pencil, bud," I said.

"Just tell me how to do it!" he protested, becoming more and more frustrated each time I asked to show him. He wanted my help. He just wanted me to communicate with him in the way he understood best.

He wanted a speaking mom, not a showing mom. So, even though it was hard for me, I did my best to explain in the way he could understand most easily.

Luckily for us, we have a God who will do the same thing for us, and we know this because He does it in Scripture.

We read in Genesis that Jacob went on to have twelve sons and loved his son Joseph more than any of the others (which is kind of funny because it's through Jacob's story that we learned God loves us all the same).

Jacob's favoritism created issues for Joseph because of his eleven jealous brothers. It also didn't help that Joseph was a dreamer.

Joseph once had a specific dream and told his brothers about it, saying, " 'Listen to this dream I had: We were binding sheaves of grain out in the field when suddenly my sheaf rose and stood upright, while your sheaves gathered around mine and bowed down to it.'

"His brothers said to him, 'Do you intend to reign over us? Will you actually rule us?' "[23]

Because of all this, his brothers hated him. They hated him so much that they planned to kill him but decided to sell him into slavery instead. Through some interesting and unfortunate circumstances, Joseph ended up in jail. Yet, even while he was in prison, the Lord continued to use dreams to speak to and through Joseph. This is the means of communication that the Lord chose to use to interact with this man. Probably because God knew this was the way Joseph would understand best. Maybe he needed to be shown and not told.

Do you know what I love about God using dreams to speak to Joseph? Joseph's father, grandfather, and great-grandfather all had recorded conversations with the Lord. God had spoken audibly to each generation of men before Joseph, but God chose to speak to Joseph through dreams and their meanings.

As parents, we are limited in the ways we can share our hearts with our children. We are limited by our own strengths and weaknesses. But God is not limited. He knows exactly how to communicate with our hearts so that we receive what He is saying. And He speaks to us in individual ways.

I think today He'd remind us, *Let Me tenderly guide your heart in the way that I know best. I might speak audibly to you or quietly prompt your heart or even give you a dream in the night. I might share with you through the voice of a friend or a song on the radio. I might reveal My heart through My creation. Don't miss My voice because you're expecting Me to speak in a certain way. If you focus on Me, you won't miss a word of what I want you to know.*

Lord, thank You for being a God who uses multiple means to make Your messages known. We will listen and look for Your voice today knowing You might communicate in unexpected ways. In Jesus's name we pray. Amen.

This Is Holy Ground

God Calls to Moses

Exodus 3

From the moment I wake up until the moment I close my eyes, I am taking care of something. It might be a person (one of my three kids or my husband); it might be my home with the endless laundry and dishes; it might be the stack of bills that just keep coming in the mail. I might be busy answering emails or planning the rest of my week or just thinking ahead to dinner. I might be busy taking care of the smelly hamster cage or finding five minutes to take care of me. But no matter what I'm taking care of, I am in a season of constantly accomplishing something so I don't fall behind. Each moment is accounted for.

I realize that I won't always be in a season like this one. I realize that at some point, the people around me and the things on my list will require less of my attention and care. I get it. That's what every veteran mom has told me for nearly a decade. But for now, I'm still in the middle of a life that feels like work. Often joyful work . . . but work nonetheless.

It doesn't always feel like holy work either. It doesn't always feel important. It usually feels like just plain old everyday stuff—as if I'm just going from one need to the next, taking care of what's right in front of me. But that's exactly where God often intervenes. I think Moses would understand what I mean.

Moses was in a season of taking care of his father-in-law's sheep when God met him in the middle of his day. He had led his flock to the side of a mountain called Horeb when he saw a bush that was burning but was not consumed by the fire.

Scripture says that the Lord called to Moses from the bush. "Moses! Moses!"

"Here I am," Moses answered.

"'Do not come any closer,' God said. 'Take off your sandals, for the place where you are standing is holy ground. . . . I am the God of your father, the God of Abraham, the God of Isaac and the God of Jacob.' At this, Moses hid his face, because he was afraid to look at God."[24]

One minute Moses was making sure the sheep were all doing their sheep stuff. He was dodging a flock's worth of poo and making sure everyone was fed. I bet it felt a lot like motherhood, to be honest. And the next moment, the God of creation was speaking to him from a burning bush. Talk about a perspective shift. Talk about his focus being moved from taking care of what was right in front of him to what was eternal.

In our lives, so often we get focused on the tasks in front of us and we forget that the same fire in the bush burns within us. We forget that we have the opportunity to have an encounter with the living God at any point in our day. He calls to us just as He called to Adam, Abraham, Isaac, Jacob, and Moses. He invites us to speak with Him, to come close to Him, to hear His heart. The Lord is continually inviting us into a holy moment with Him, saying to each of us, *My presence makes your life holy ground. Your ordinary and busy tasks are full of holy work. Your service impacts eternity. Your love builds My kingdom. You're doing more than you realize as you care for those around you, because through it all you're revealing My heart.*

What if in the middle of everything else, we stopped to remember that we carry holy ground wherever we go? It just might change our perspective. It just might change how we feel about where we go and what we do and how we carefully guide little sheep.

Lord, help us remember Your continual presence as we face each task in front of us. Help us see it as holy work. Help us realize the impact our lives will have on eternity. Help us commit our daily assignments to building Your kingdom. In Jesus's name we pray. Amen.

I AM

God Speaks to Moses

Exodus 3

I love my children fiercely, but there are plenty of moments when I wonder what God was thinking when He decided that I was the best person to raise them. Do you ever feel this way? Sure, there are times when I think, *YES! I handled that so well! I'm amazing.* But I would be dishonest if I led you to believe that there aren't just as many moments when I wonder, *What made You think that I could do this, God? I mean, clearly I'm ruining these kids for life. You see how I'm not the right person for this assignment?*

Our hearts can flip so easily, can't they? We can jump from completely confident to completely discouraged in no time at all. But what does God say to us in moments like these?

When we look over Scripture, we find that God shows up when we suddenly become unsure of His assignments. Let's revisit the moment that God spoke to Moses from the burning bush. Let's pause to consider how Moses might have felt in this exact space. Can you imagine how you would feel? The God who created the universe revealed Himself as fire and spoke audibly to Moses from a plant. I mean . . . What?!

Aside from the reverence and the revelation of his own sinfulness, I'm sure that as Moses came close to God, he thought, *God is here with me! This is amazing! BEST day ever!* At least, that's how I would have felt.

But then God began to speak. He tasked Moses with the assignment to go back to Egypt and free His people from bondage.

And just like that, Moses went from seeing this great sight to carrying this great assignment. Do you suppose he felt an enormous emotional shift? Do you suppose he went from sure of himself to questioning everything? We can see his uncertainty in his response to God.

Moses answered the Lord, "Who am I that I should go to Pharaoh and bring the Israelites out of Egypt?"[25]

He sounds like me. "Umm. Who am I to take on this assignment? Me? Are You sure? You really thought I could do this?"

But God answers us with the same words He replied to Moses.

"I will be with you."[26]

See, here's the thing. The freedom that Moses would bring to the Israelites wasn't proof of Moses's abilities. It was proof of God's faithfulness. The same is true as God gives us the assignment to care for our families. What we do for our children and our husbands and how we lead and love others isn't proof of our ability. What God assigns to us isn't proof of what He thinks we can do on our own. It is proof of what God wants to accomplish through us. Each assignment given to us by God is proof of His faithfulness to lead as we turn and love others.

When we find ourselves in moments of questioning and wondering, *Who am I that I should be able to do any of this?* I believe God says, *Don't you see? This isn't about you. Your position in your family and this assignment I've given you are opportunities for Me to reveal My presence and My goodness to your children through you. I am here to reveal who I am and that I am enough. I am faithful. I am with you. I am everything your family needs, and I am asking you to carry My love and let Me do the rest.*

It's normal to wonder if we can really do what God calls us to do. But each time we doubt, we should listen closely, because the voice of the Father is reminding us that He is more than enough.

Lord, thank You for each area of our lives in which we feel inadequate because these moments reveal Your strength. Train our hearts to tune to Your voice as You remind us again and again that You are enough. In Jesus's name we pray. Amen.

Look at Your Hands

God Equips Moses

Exodus 4

---

*H*ave you ever had one of those moments where you realize your kid is acting just like you? Maybe she's being particularly sassy or strong willed or determined. Maybe he's being compassionate or comedic or critical. I have noticed that my children in this season are crystal-clear mirrors of who I am as a person. Sometimes this is good, and sometimes it reveals the places where I need to spend a little more time developing my character (or my dance moves).

I can say this: each of my children has unique personality traits that I remember working through when I was younger, and because I've already dealt with these situations, I can help them. It's almost as if I went through them just so I could help my kids. I believe God was preparing me for these moments long before they arrived. He had placed tools in my hands, and I hadn't realized what they were.

This is exactly what God revealed to Moses. When God spoke to Moses out of the burning bush and commissioned him to take on the assignment of a lifetime, Moses offered every excuse for why he wasn't the right guy to ask. Moses didn't think anyone would believe that God had sent him. He wanted to hear

God's name. He wanted to know God would be with him. Moses wanted affirmation that God knew what He was doing.

To prove that Moses was equipped, the Lord asked him, "What is that in your hand?"

"A staff," he replied.[27]

I'm sure Moses was thinking, *What do You mean? It's the stick that I use to walk and lead the sheep and climb mountains.*

"The Lord said, 'Throw it on the ground.'

"Moses threw it on the ground and it became a snake, and he ran from it. Then the Lord said to him, 'Reach out your hand and take it by the tail.' So Moses reached out and took hold of the snake and it turned back into a staff in his hand. 'This,' said the Lord, 'is so that they may believe that the Lord, the God of their fathers—the God of Abraham, the God of Isaac and the God of Jacob—has appeared to you.'"[28]

This staff wasn't just any stick Moses had chosen off the ground. It wasn't a stick from the burning bush. It was the stick that Moses had held in his hand daily. And God used this stick to be the sign to all those who needed to believe that God was with Moses and was on his side.

God has always been in the business of taking what's already in our hands and using it supernaturally to accomplish His purposes.

Everything that we have been through has been preparing us to take on everything else that God is asking us to do from here. Each mountain and valley was training us to become this mom to these kids.

God takes what we have used in the past—our skills, talents, and giftings and the special characteristics of our lives—to help us lead and love our families.

Just like Moses, when we offer the Lord what we already have in our hands, He supernaturally transforms it for His purposes.

I believe the Lord is asking us both today, *What's in your hand, daughter? What's already there? You thought that it was only used for one thing, but what you have learned in the fields while taking care of the sheep will be what I use to prove My presence and My power. Offer Me what is in your hand, and I'll give you what is in Mine instead.*

We have access to God's unlimited strength and resources. We just need to bring the offering of our lives before Him and watch as He uses what He has already placed within us for His glory.

Lord, thank You for placing within us gifts and talents and characteristics that You can use to bring love to Your people and glory to Your name. Help us see the value of what You've already given us. In Jesus's name we pray. Amen.

Help Is on the Way

God Tells Moses That Aaron Will Help

Exodus 4

My heart raced. My palms were sweaty. I was face-to-face with one of my worst fears. I was in the middle of a crowded lunchroom, surrounded by people I did not know, without a place to sit or a friend in the world.

We moved a lot when I was younger. And at each new school, I would avoid the cafeteria like the plague. For a year, I walked home every day to eat lunch by myself instead of having to face the crowded cafeteria. At another school, I chose to eat on a quiet bench instead of having to find a seat with everyone else.

But my junior year of high school, there would be no avoiding it. I would be confronted with one of the most uncomfortable scenarios I could imagine, and it wasn't because I disliked being around other people. It was because I loved being around other people. *I just could not imagine anything worse than feeling unwanted or unwelcome.*

I wasn't alone for long. A kind girl in my Spanish class invited me to sit with her. I've thought about that simple conversation a lot over the last ten-plus years. Because there have been more moments in my life when I have felt like I am still the kid wandering through the cafeteria with a tray in her hand and no place to put it down, wishing that God would send someone to help me again. Maybe you've felt that way too. Maybe you just want to hear that you're not going to go through this alone.

You know, when God tasked Moses with going back for the Israelites to free them from Pharaoh, it felt like too great an assignment to do alone. Moses had many questions. Who shall I say sent me?[29] What if they don't believe me? What if they *still* don't believe me? Finally, Moses said, "Pardon your servant, Lord. Please send someone else."[30]

When it came down to it, Moses was afraid that who he was wouldn't be enough to take on the assignment God had given him.

But the Lord didn't withdraw the assignment. Instead, the Lord answered, "What about your brother, Aaron the Levite? I know he can speak well. He is already on his way to meet you, and he will be glad to see you. You shall speak to him and put words in his mouth; I will help both of you speak and will teach you what to do. He will speak to the people for you, and it will be as if he were your mouth and as if you were God to him. But take this staff in your hand so you can perform the signs with it."[31]

God didn't send someone in Moses's place. No, God sent Aaron to meet Moses before Moses even asked for Aaron's help. God had a plan for exactly who would come alongside him and the call on his life.

The truth is, God sends people into each of our lives before we even reach the place where we feel as though we cannot do it alone. He sends helpers to find us sitting along the walls of cafeterias and on mountainsides. God sends people to find us when we feel as though we aren't equipped to take on the tasks right in front of us. When deep in our hearts we say, *Can't You just send someone else, God?*

And He answers, *I won't send someone to do it for you, but I can send someone to do it with you. I can send you help. The women you will lean on aren't as far away as you think. This task I've given you feels like a lot, but help is coming. You won't always have to do this alone. I'm sending people to love and encourage and welcome you fully into their lives even now.*

Maybe you are starting a new job or have moved to a new town. Maybe you are a mommy who spends her days taking care of little ones and you are desperate for friendship. You wonder where you will fit in or if you will be welcome. For those of us at home or on a bench or against the wall, we aren't unseen. Today hold on to this hope. Help is on the way.

Lord, remind us that You delight in being our strength and that You understand our need to have others come alongside us and support us. Strengthen us so we do not lose heart as we wait for help, and guide us to become the help for others that we desire in our own lives. In Jesus's name. Amen.

I Keep My Promises

God Sends a Message to Israel

Exodus 5

I don't think there is anything the Enemy loves more than a discouraged mom. Do you know why? Because the Enemy knows how vital a mother's personal hope is to the level of hope present in her home. I'm sure you've experienced this in your own life. When you're stressed or overwhelmed or discouraged, your whole family feels it. Everyone seems a little off. Everything seems less peaceful.

So the Enemy does all he can to discourage us and keep us so busy that we don't even have time to focus on or hear the voice of Truth in our lives. How do I know this is true?

We see this play out with the Israelites. God sent Moses and Aaron to bring the Israelites out of bondage and into a place where they could freely worship God. When Pharaoh heard Moses's request, he made life for the Israelites harder. Pharaoh said, "Make the work harder for the people so that they keep working and pay no attention to lies."[32] This was his intentional plan to distract the Israelites.

In other words, "If we make them so busy, they won't be concerned with the hope that has come. If we make them more burdened, they will be too discouraged to think of anything else." This is what the Enemy does to us as well. "Make them more burdened! Make them more stressed! Make them focused more on their circumstances and how impossible they feel rather than on the hope that is available to them."

God had come with this message for His people: "I am the LORD, and I will bring you out from under the yoke of the Egyptians. I will free you from being slaves to them, and I will redeem you with an outstretched arm and with mighty acts of judgment. . . . I am the LORD."[33]

But when Moses and Aaron came to the people and told them, Scripture says, "They did not listen to him because of their discouragement and harsh labor."[34] They were too discouraged to hear the Truth.

What a nasty trick! The Israelites had been in bondage to the Egyptians for generations. They had been waiting centuries for a deliverer. But their enemy had them so overwhelmed, exhausted, and defeated that they were unable to receive the message of the Lord. They were unable to even hear that Hope had come for them.

I'm not guilty of this daily, but there have definitely been times when I have focused more on my discouragement than on the voice of Hope in my life. There have been times when my busyness and exhaustion kept me doing what was right in front of me rather than listening to the voice of my Father inviting me away to worship Him and spend time in His presence.

Is this ever true for you? Because I believe if we listen closely we will hear the Father speaking hope over our hearts right now. I believe we will hear Him saying, *I will bring you out of this. I am your Lord. Come away and spend time with Me. Come away from the heaviness of your heart. Let Me take your dis-*

couragement as I shift your circumstances. I am the Lord and I remember the promises that I have made to you.

When we become aware of the Enemy's strategies, we are able to overcome them. We aren't just fighting against flesh and blood and personal circumstances; we are fighting against what would steal our joy, our patience, and our love. Today, let's remember the Truth that the Lord came to deliver us from this type of hopelessness.

Lord, thank You for being the God of hope. We know that You desire us to be full of Your love and Your hope so that we can lead and love our families well. God, You spoil the plans of the Enemy, and You bring us out from defeat. Break discouragement off our lives, God. Tune our hearts to Your Truth. In Jesus's name we pray. Amen.

I'll Prepare You for Transition

God Tells the Israelites to Get Ready to Leave Egypt

Exodus 12

The Lord called us to move to Los Angeles in February, but we didn't actually pull out of town until early December. We had a long period of time to prepare our hearts for what was coming. In contrast, I have a friend who found out that her husband was being transferred and they would be moving in less than a month.

I'm not sure which of us had a harder transition. We had a slow process of realizing what we were leaving behind, how much our lives were going to change, and exactly what this transition meant. It was a long emotional process. My friend spent the few weeks she had scrambling to make arrangements and working out all the details. Our transitions were hard for very different reasons. The good news is that the Lord saw us, cared about both of us, and helped us through our shifting seasons in very personal and yet very different ways. Because He is a God who works with us through our transitions.

The Israelites leaving Egypt is an incredible picture of God transitioning His people from one season to the next. When Moses asked Pharaoh to allow the Israelites to leave and go worship their God in the desert, Pharaoh refused, and God sent plagues. There were ten in total, but God knew that the final plague would move Pharaoh's heart. After hundreds of years in slavery, God knew the exact night that the Israelites would be released by Pharaoh.

He told the Israelites this: "I will pass through Egypt and strike down every firstborn of both people and animals, and I will bring judgment on all the gods of Egypt. I am the Lord."[35]

So that the Israelites might be spared, God said, "Each man is to take a lamb for his family. . . . Take some of the blood and put it on the sides and tops of the doorframes of the houses where they eat the lambs. . . . This is how you are to eat it: with your cloak tucked into your belt, your sandals on your feet and your staff in your hand. Eat it in haste; it is the Lord's Passover. . . . When I see the blood, I will pass over you. No destructive plague will touch you when I strike Egypt."[36]

Those are very thorough directions, but God had a purpose for each part. We see a beautiful foreshadowing that Passover night of what Jesus would do for us on the cross. Just as the blood of perfect lambs, when it was applied to the doors in Egypt, saved the Israelites, the sacrifice of Jesus spares us from death when His shed blood is applied to our lives.

God had another reason for giving the Israelites such detailed instructions. They were supposed to eat with their cloaks in their belts. They were supposed to eat with their shoes on their feet and their staffs in their hands. They were supposed to eat the meal and be ready to go because God knew when the angel passed over in the night, Pharaoh would tell them to leave.

This is exactly what happened. In the middle of the night, Pharaoh summoned Moses and Aaron and said, "Up! Leave my people, you and the Israelites! Go, worship the Lord as you have requested. Take your flocks and herds, as you have said, and go."[37]

And when it was time for the Israelites to leave, even though it happened suddenly, they were ready because the Lord had prepared them. He cared about their transition just as He cares about ours. Sometimes we don't feel ready when life shifts suddenly, but God has been preparing our hearts.

I believe He says to us, *Change doesn't surprise Me. It doesn't come suddenly to Me. I know the exact moment everything will change. I want you to trust Me through the process. I want you to see that I not only know when, but I also know how and where and why and what. I have seen the other side of this road ahead of you, and I have been getting you ready for this, whether you realized I was or not. You are more equipped than you realize.*

God doesn't just wait for us on the other side of where we are. He is like the dad who helps us tie our shoes and put on our coats and then takes our hands to walk us safely to the place He has already prepared.

Lord, help us listen to the instructions You give even when they don't make any sense to us, so when You say, "It's time!" we are ready. In Jesus's name we pray. Amen.

There's a Reason I Brought You This Way

God Directs the Israelites

Exodus 13

Have you ever wondered why God brought you this way? I don't just mean right now, today. I mean in your life journey. Do you ever look around and think, *Why has God led me here? Why is this part of my story? Why did we go through that? Why are we going through this now? Why this way, Lord?*

Whether it is our kids or our marriages, our families or our friends, our ministries or our assignments, there are plenty of opportunities to say to ourselves, *God, I know You're faithful to lead me, but what is the purpose in this part of the path?*

Before we consider the why, we need to recognize that every step God directs us to take is carefully calculated. And sometimes He has us take steps in one direction so we won't take steps in another. The Israelites' journey out of Egypt is proof of this.

The day the Israelites left Egypt, God took them the long way. All that time in bondage, and as they embarked on their journey to freedom, God did not lead them down the shortest path to their Promised Land. Scripture says, "When

Pharaoh let the people go, God did not lead them on the road through the Philistine country, though that was shorter. For God said, 'If they face war, they might change their minds and return to Egypt.'"[38]

God knew the hearts of the Israelites. He knew that if He led them the shortest way through Philistine territory and they faced war, they would become discouraged and would perhaps return to Egypt. He loved them too much to let that happen. He loved them too much to let them go back into bondage. He loved them too much to take them the short way where they might face an early defeat and return to what was familiar.

So He led the people around by the desert road toward the Red Sea. He led them the long way.

Sometimes God sees things in us that we might not see or recognize in ourselves. God recognized what the Israelites had been through. They were journeying toward freedom, but they had been through so much already. He said, "If they face war, they might change their minds and return to Egypt." God wasn't just planning for what would happen. He was planning for what could happen. He was planning for how the Israelites might feel.

Do you see how this impacts us? God isn't just planning for what we will do. He is planning for what we might do. We might change our minds. We might turn around. We might become discouraged. We might want to go back to what is familiar. We might turn to something other than His presence when we face difficulty. And God loves us so much that He is looking ahead and seeing the places where things could go wrong, and then He is course correcting on this side of it before we even get there. God loves us so much He is even planning for our maybes.

Sometimes I get so caught up in wondering why I'm going through certain things in my life that I miss the opportunity to thank God for seeing what I can't and for loving me enough to make sure I'm on this road instead of another. I miss the chance to thank God for the road He did not lead me down.

I ask, *Why are we taking the long way, God? Why are we here?* And God answers me, *I have seen the other path, and I have chosen this to be the safest route. There's a reason that we're taking what feels to be the long way through this. There's a reason you're not over there. There's a reason I'm walking you carefully down this road and not the other. I love you too much to allow you to take the short road. I love you too much to let you slip away from the best that I have for you.*

Praise the Lord that He loves us enough to calculate our feelings into His perfect plan.

Lord, thank You for knowing our hearts better than we do. Thank You for the kind of love that leads us the long way. In Jesus's name we pray. Amen.

I Can Do the Impossible

God Tells Moses to Part the Red Sea

Exodus 14

---

*I*t was always possible. There was always a way. God could always do it. The only thing that changed was our perspective. When God called us to California, we had no idea how He was going to make a way for it to become a reality. We didn't have the money. We didn't have jobs. We had no answers to the question, *How will You accomplish this, God?* We just had the confidence that God had said, *"Go."* And we had the faith to start walking even without the full plan revealed. So we sold our house before we even had a chance to secure a rental property across the country or figure out how we were going to pay for it. I know you might not be moving across the country. But if I had to guess, I'd say you have been in a situation where you thought, *God, what happens now? Because I just don't see it.*

If there was ever a group of people who understood impossible circumstances, it was the Israelites. When God called them out of Egypt and began to lead them to their Promised Land, they made it to the edge of the Red Sea and everything seemed to be over. The Egyptians were closing in on the Israelites; hundreds of thousands were trapped. They had the sea in front of them and the Egyptian army behind them, and they were out of options.

Moses went to the Lord and asked what to do. God answered, "Why are you crying out to me? Tell the Israelites to move on. Raise your staff and stretch out your hand over the sea to divide the water so that the Israelites can go through the sea on dry ground."[39]

I love God's tone in this passage. "Why are you crying out to Me? Just hold out your hand and split the sea and then go across."

Oh, right, God. Of course. I should have known . . . the sea was going to part. Gotcha. Don't know why I didn't think of that myself.

To God it was just so obvious. It was just what was going to happen next, because God already knew that He was a sea-splitting God. He already knew what was possible.

"Moses stretched out his hand over the sea, and all that night the LORD drove the sea back with a strong east wind and turned it into dry land. The waters were divided, and the Israelites went through the sea on dry ground, with a wall of water on their right and on their left."[40]

Done. Easy. Nearly a million people crossed the Red Sea, and the Egyptians drowned in the process of pursuing them. It was just another part of the supernatural deliverance of God's people.

But the Israelites didn't know a sea could part until it did. They didn't know God was able until He did it. It doesn't mean that God was unable before they saw it; they just came into a new understanding of what God could do.

For our part, we don't even know how God is going to get us out of our personal situations until He does. However, He's not surprised by His power and His abilities, and we shouldn't be either. We should always be looking for seas to part in the presence of the God who holds it all together with His Word. We should always expect the Lord to intervene in a supernatural way. In fear, we might be calling out, "Don't you see that we're out of options here, God?!" And I believe He'd say to us something similar to what He said to Moses: *Why are you crying out to Me? Hold up your hands and worship the God who you know can do anything. Don't you know that I didn't bring you here to forget about you? Don't you know that I can use the breath of My Holy Spirit to blow across your circumstances and rearrange what seems impossibly solid? There is a way, because I am the Way.*

While the Israelites didn't even know it was possible for the waters to part, we have the benefit of knowing that if God can split the sea, He can do anything for us. Watch and wait, friend. He is able.

Lord, there's nothing too difficult for You. Help us remember this when the small details of our lives seem so big. Train us to see opportunities for You to break into our ordinary lives in extraordinary ways. In Jesus's name we pray. Amen.

Store Up My Faithfulness

God Tells the Israelites to Keep a Jar of His Provision

Exodus 16

A few years ago, I started thanking God out loud at the grocery store in front of my children. As we unload the food onto the belt and the cashier begins to scan and bag our groceries, I say, "Thank You, Lord, that we had enough money to buy all this wonderful food. Thank You for the jobs that give us the money to buy the meals. Thank You, God, for taking care of us in this way. Help us remember to take care of others."

Honestly, it's easy to forget to be thankful not just for what we have but for the One who gave us what we have. When those daily blessings are all part of the stressful routine of life, it's easy to overlook them. I want to train my children to see God providing in the most ordinary ways.

This is the type of legacy I want to leave for my children. I want them to see everything that we have as a gift that came from God because of His good love for us. And I want them to be inspired to give to others because they are aware of how much they have been given. I want this awareness to compel them to take care of others as a way of extending God's love and provision through us.

In our home, this generosity begins with a reminder of the One who gives. This provision is something the Lord never wants His people to forget.

When the Israelites were wandering the desert for forty years, the Lord supernaturally provided food for them each morning. Scripture says that the ground would be covered with white flakes of bread that looked like coriander seeds but were sweet like honey. Each morning, they were to collect a jar for each member of their family. They were never to collect more than they needed. If they did, it would spoil before they could eat it. God did this to teach the Israelites to trust Him daily for their provision.

I mean, can you imagine having to eat the same food every day for forty years? Personally, I hate leftovers after about the third meal of them. But as the Israelites wandered in the wilderness, it wasn't just bread they were given; they received God's love literally poured out as a meal every morning.

God told the people, "Take an omer [jar] of manna and keep it for the generations to come, so they can see the bread I gave you to eat in the wilderness when I brought you out of Egypt."[41]

So they did. They collected a daily jar of food and kept a jar just to remember God's gracious provision so they could tell their children and their grandchildren what God had done and then show them proof of it.

You know, perhaps the Lord would have us do the same. Perhaps He'd say, *Store up the moments of My faithfulness. Keep a record so that your children and your grandchildren will know that I am good. It is possible to overlook My daily provision because you have come to expect it. It is possible to miss the joy of the blessing because it is so common. But like the Israelites filled a jar with manna, I want you to fill a jar with the testimonies of My faithfulness to you and your family.*

What a great reminder. Are we writing down what He has done for us? Are we stopping to point out each moment of His lavish love displayed in the most basic ways to our children? Or are we just consuming it daily, not stopping to marvel at the miracle of His persistent provision?

I don't just want to tell my children stories one day. I want to have a jar full of moments for them to hold on to.

Lord, thank You for each blessing in our lives. Help us stop to thank the One who provides rather than just take the gift for granted. Help us teach our children to expect Your faithful provision but to still marvel with gratefulness every time it comes. In Jesus's name. Amen.

Boundaries Reveal My Love

God Gives the Israelites the Law

*J*ust don't go out toward the field! The stickers are out there!"

If you're from the Midwest, you likely know exactly what I mean when I say stickers. In case you're less familiar with this term, stickers are seeds. But these aren't just any seeds. They are sharp on all sides, and they stick to your shoes and clothes. They also stick painfully to unsuspecting feet.

When we lived in Oklahoma, we did our best to find these weeds in our yard and pull them up before our kids stepped on them. However, since the seeds spread so easily, we were always fighting them. As a mom, I was constantly worried that tiny toes would find their way into a sticker patch.

Thankfully the stickers were mostly around the edges of the property, and to keep the kids safe, we gave them very clear boundaries. Yet they would often try to venture out toward the edge anyway. "Why can't we go any farther?" they'd occasionally ask. "I don't see any stickers!" And we would do our best to remind them that we kept them closer to us to keep them from getting hurt. This is what any good parent would do.

This is what God did for the Israelites and what He continues to do for us today. After the Israelites came out of Egypt and began to follow the Lord, God called Moses up the mountain and gave him commandments by which the people of God should live.

God said to Moses, "I am the LORD your God, who brought you out of Egypt, out of the land of slavery."[42]

God gave His people the Ten Commandments and went on to give them 613 laws in total. Talk about clear boundaries!

The good news for us today is that these laws were fulfilled through Jesus. John said, "For the law was given through Moses; grace and truth came through Jesus Christ."[43] While it might take the rest of our Christian walk to fully appreciate what that means, today we can all agree that every rule God gave and every boundary He puts in place in our lives are not to limit us but to help us and to keep us safe.

Many who don't understand our faith ask why our God seems to be so cruel, preventing His people from enjoying certain things. But we know our Lord as a kind Father. We know that He didn't set boundaries to keep His people from enjoying certain things or to limit them. He set these rules in place to protect them and to give them the strategy to live their best lives.

As parents, the rules we set before our kids are not always fun to enforce. As a matter of fact, requiring my children to obey what I have said is one of my least favorite parts of parenting. The process of bending wills and not breaking them, part of the unceasing job of making sure we follow through with what we have asked our kids to do, is mentally and emotionally exhausting. But when we set boundaries in place for little feet, and we set rules in place for growing kids, and we set clear limits for our teenagers, it's never to hinder their joy but to foster it in a healthy environment. And every rule proves our love.

As adults, we know this is true of God's love for us. We know that God places boundaries in our lives not to restrict, but to reveal His wisdom and love, knowing what's best for us. Yet often we tiptoe to the edge and say, "But why? What's the harm in it? Why aren't You letting me go where I want to go? Why can't I do what I want to do? Why are You keeping this from me?"

And God responds to us with what we would say to our own kids: *Don't you see how much I love you? Don't you see why I kept you from it? Don't you understand why I required your obedience in that area? I have so much good for you. I have such a higher perspective. I am aware of every danger and pitfall. I can see every opportunity for joy. I ask you to follow Me because My boundaries reveal My love for you.*

When we think of God's hand in our lives from the perspective of a loving parent rather than a curious child, we see just how intentional He is in loving and guiding us.

Lord, sometimes we still question why. This week, would You help us see the boundaries in our lives as safety guides rather than restrictions? Remind us of Your good love. In Jesus's name we pray. Amen.

Don't Hold Your Breath

God Tells the Israelites to Shout

Joshua 6
---

*I*was standing in the bathroom, preparing myself for what was coming later that day. I had to leave for an appointment, and having just moved, my kids still felt more comfortable with momma at home. So I wasn't just getting ready to leave or getting ready for the time I'd spend in my meeting. I was preparing my heart for how my children would respond to all of it. Would there be tears? Would they beg me to stay? As I dabbed on a little mascara, I told the Lord, *I feel like I'm just holding my breath, waiting to see how this is all going to turn out.*

And so clearly, I heard Him reply, *Don't. Don't hold your breath. Use it.*

Use it? I wondered as I put on the rest of my makeup.

I wasn't the first person God had given this message to. When the Israelites came to the city of Jericho, a walled city, the Lord spoke to Joshua and gave him specific instructions on how to overthrow it.

The Lord said, "See, I have delivered Jericho into your hands, along with its king and its fighting men. March around the city once with all the armed men. Do this for six days. Have seven priests carry trumpets of rams' horns in front of the ark. On the seventh day, march around the city seven times, with the priests blowing the trumpets. When you hear them sound a long blast on the trumpets, have the whole army give a loud shout; then the wall of the city will collapse and the army will go up, everyone straight in."[44]

The Israelites did just as God commanded and the walls fell down. The voices of the Israelites carried power because their obedience revealed their trust in God. Their shout decreed, "We believe You are who You say You are. We believe You will do what You say You will do."

Scripture tells us to be anxious for nothing but with thanksgiving to present our requests to God.[45] While patience and waiting on the Lord are important, there are certain situations where we need to remember that God has given us the authority to impact the world around us. He doesn't want us to wait and see how things play out when He has called us to conquer it and take it for His kingdom. He wants us to use our voices. He wants us to pray and ask Him to intervene, believing that He will.

So often we walk around holding our breath, uncertain about our future. We are holding our breath, waiting to see how a certain situation unfolds. We are holding our breath, waiting to see who our children will become as a result of our parenting. We are holding our breath waiting to see if we were good moms or good wives or enough in the eyes of our grown kids, our husbands, and our friends.

But the Lord doesn't want us to simply hold our breath, worried about our future, when He says that He has given us the power to change it.

The Lord is asking us to lift up a shout to Him. He's telling us, *Don't hold your breath. Use it. Don't anxiously wait. Confidently pray with a thankful heart and present your requests to Me, knowing that I will respond and be exactly who you need Me to be in every situation. Daughter, your voice is far too valuable to hold your breath.*

What would you pray if you knew the Lord was on your side? What would you conquer in confidence rather than dread in fear? What would you use your voice to accomplish for the kingdom?

Lord, we know that we have the choice to live in slight dread of what is coming or live in the sure confidence that You desire to intervene. Help us remember to bring all things before You as we confidently declare that You are ready to come to our aid in even the smallest situations. In Jesus's name we pray. Amen.

Your Prayers Are Powerful

God Responds to Hannah

1 Samuel 1

I was in the middle of working on my first book to encourage moms when I received a photo message from my own momma. It was a photograph of a page of her journal, and in my momma's cursive handwriting was written, "I pray for the new baby that he/she would be a testimony to Your love and power to sustain parents especially moms through hard times and trials."

It took me a minute to understand what I was reading.

Before I was born, before my mom even knew if she was having a boy or a girl, she prayed very specific prayers for her baby . . . for me. She had prayed that I would be a testimony of God's love and power to sustain moms through hard times and trials. And there I was literally living the fulfillment of her prayer, while holding proof of her prayer in my hands. It was mind blowing and humbling, and it sent me to my knees, praying for my own children.

My mom couldn't have known what was coming for her baby. She couldn't have known that someday I'd start a blog and write mom books. She couldn't have known that God would call me to this specific work, but God knew, and He heard her. And perhaps He was the One who placed that prayer in her heart in the first place over thirty years ago.

If I'm being honest, I pray for my children, but I worry about them more. Jesus taught in Matthew 6:27, "Can any one of you by worrying add a single hour to your life?" The easy answer is obviously no. We cannot add to our lives or our children's lives by worrying about them, but we add tremendously to the lives of our children by praying for them. Prayer takes what we cannot control and hands it over to the Lord, inviting Him to do what only He can with it. A mom should never underestimate the power of her prayers.

Hannah is one woman in Scripture who exemplifies this profoundly. Unable to have children, Hannah prayed to the Lord, weeping bitterly. And she made a vow, saying, "LORD Almighty, if you will only look on your servant's misery and remember me, and not forget your servant but give her a son, then I will give him to the LORD for all the days of his life, and no razor will ever be used on his head."[46]

The priest saw Hannah praying without using words and thought she was drunk. When she explained what she was doing, the priest said, "Go in peace, and may the God of Israel grant you what you have asked of him."[47]

Scripture says that in due time Hannah had a son and dedicated his life to the Lord.

Sometimes we pray without words, and sometimes God answers us without words. And when Hannah gave birth to a baby boy, it was as if God said to her, *"I heard you."*

The Lord heard Hannah. The Lord heard my mom. And the Lord hears you and me too. I don't know what you're believing for, I don't know what you have prayed and forgotten about, but I promise God heard, He remembers, and He is bringing it all together in His time.

Where the world presents moments to worry, God says, *Invite Me to be a part of your parenting. Invite Me to do what only I can with your kids. Ask for My purpose and destiny for them. Pray the words that I place on your heart. Pray believing that I love your children more than you do, and I want to bless them.*

And friend? Don't forget to write your prayers down, because you might just read them thirty years from now and realize the significance of every word.

Lord, thank You for being the God who hears us. Thank You for loving our kids. Thank You for teaching us how and what to pray for our children. Help us remember that we cannot add to their lives by worrying, but we can add to their lives by lifting them up to You. In Jesus's name we pray. Amen.

Can I Say Something?

God Calls Samuel

---

1 Samuel 3

I will be honest. Sometimes I just need to talk things out. Do you know anyone else who is like this? Occasionally I will find that when everything feels like it's too much or I'm caught on some crazy carousel of anxious or unproductive thinking, I need to call a friend or my mom and just say, "Here's what's going on." I have a few healthy relationships in which I know if I consult wise counsel, they will point me back to the Word and end our conversation with a prayer.

But in my life, I have learned that I am not just interested in finding a solution to my problems. I am almost equally interested in the process of sharing my heart as I am in receiving good advice. Okay. Let's be real. Sometimes I care way more about telling all my problems than actually hearing what I should do about them.

This is where communication often breaks down between my husband and me. My husband is an advice giver. He is ready with at least one great solution whether or not I'm ready to hear it. He doesn't care that I wanted to tell him about my entire day, and he's giving me solutions at the 3 p.m. mark in my story. I don't want answers. I want him to hear me! "But you haven't heard the worst of it!" I always say.

Sometimes we just need someone to listen. But I think if we're not careful we can get caught in this same conversation trap with the Lord. We expect Him to do most of the listening while we just share everything that's bothering us.

But can you imagine if you had the opportunity to walk into a room right now and speak to Jesus face-to-face? What if you went in, spent an hour talking, and walked out, never pausing to hear what He had to say in return? That'd be ridiculous.

We can spend so much time telling God what's going on that we forget to create a space in our hearts to hear Him. God loves it when we share our hearts with Him, but I believe He loves it just as much when we listen for His voice and respond to what He has to say. So my question for us today is this: How much of your prayer life is spent listening?

The ability to hear God doesn't just require a God who speaks. It requires hearts that hear. If God is willing to talk to us, why don't we spend more time in His presence just listening?

There is a story in Scripture about Hannah's son, named Samuel. She had promised to give this child to the Lord since He heard her cry, and she kept her word. Even though Samuel was very young, Hannah had taken him to be raised at the temple.

One night, Samuel heard God calling him, but he didn't recognize the voice as belonging to the Lord. Instead, he thought it was the voice of his mentor, Eli. Samuel asked Eli, "Have you been calling for me?"

"Eli told Samuel, 'Go and lie down, and if he calls you, say, "Speak, LORD, for your servant is listening.""'[48]

Perhaps this is sound advice for our lives as well. Perhaps in a world that is so full of noise, we just need to stop, quiet our hearts, and say, "Your servant is listening." I believe the Lord is saying to us through this passage of Scripture, *I have been calling to you since you were young. I have been chasing down your heart so I can talk to you since you were born. Do you hear Me calling you by name? I have so much I want to say to you. Are you listening?*

Lord, we stop to listen for Your voice without an agenda, without petitions, without any purpose other than to hear You speak. And God, just as You replied to Samuel saying, "Samuel! Samuel!" we know that you're calling our names right now. We are eager to spend time getting to know Your voice better today. In Jesus's name we pray. Amen.

Give What You Have Left

God Tells the Widow to Feed Elijah

---

1 Kings 17

I signed us up to bring a meal to that family in the church," my husband said when he got home from service. "You did what?" I probably should have sounded grateful that my overly generous husband volunteered us to help a family in need, but I had stayed home from church that Sunday because I already had so much to do.

I was in a season of barely keeping my head above water. Making my own family a meal was my least favorite thing to do, and he had gone and signed us up to make a meal for someone else. I was less than enthusiastic.

"What should I make? What night am I supposed to bring it? Do they have any allergies? Diet restrictions? What is everyone else bringing?"

Jared sort of shrugged his shoulders and said, "I just thought it would be nice."

He was right. It was nice. And in any other season, I would have willingly volunteered myself. But my husband had said that I could give to someone else when I felt like I could barely give to my own family.

Listen. This is not my favorite story to tell. I wish that I could say I was more generous or eager to help. But I think many of us can agree that motherhood requires so much sacrifice, and sometimes we find ourselves in seasons where we have nothing left to offer. For me, this opportunity to serve landed itself in my lap right about the time that my lap was overflowing with everyone and everything else. Have you ever felt this way? I imagine this is exactly how a woman living in a town called Zarephath felt when a prophet named Elijah asked her to prepare a meal too.

Famine had come to land, and to provide for Elijah, God directed him to go and find a certain woman living in a place called Zarephath. When Elijah arrived, he found this woman out gathering sticks so she could make a fire and use the last of her flour and oil to bake a final meal for herself and her son. She was literally out of food, and God told her through Elijah to make the prophet something to eat. Can you imagine?

Elijah told her, "For this is what the LORD, the God of Israel says: 'The jar of flour will not be used up and the jug of oil will not run dry until the day the LORD sends rain on the land.'"

She did as Elijah told her, and as a result, there was always enough food for Elijah and for her and her family. The jar of flour was never empty and the jug of oil never ran out, just as the LORD had promised.[49]

When the woman had nothing left to give, God used what she did have and created an opportunity for her to serve someone else in the process.

Because she was willing to listen to the Lord, He made sure she had all her needs met as well.

I can't tell you how many times I have wished that someone would just show up on my porch with a casserole or volunteer to sit with my kids while I take care of the things I just don't have time for. But sometimes God says to us, *Be the one to show up for someone else in need. Give what you have left. Go help that new* mom who just had a baby. *Go take that kid to soccer practice so his momma can rest today. Offer to watch your friend's kids (in addition to yours) so that she and her husband can work on their marriage. Be the woman you wished you had in your life. Give what you have. Help when you can. And I'll make sure you and your family are taken care of as well.*

In seasons when we have nothing, our sacrifice is worth so much more. The beautiful truth is that the Lord honors it and blesses our offering.

Lord, we want to be generous. We want to give to others, but sometimes it's all we can do to take care of our own. Show us opportunities to offer what we can, when we can, knowing that You will take care of our needs in return. In Jesus's name we pray. Amen.

Sometimes I Whisper

God Speaks to Elijah

1 Kings 19

I remember one particularly hard afternoon a few years ago. I felt terrible, I was sure I was the worst mom on earth. I sat down on my couch and closed my eyes, desperately trying to recalibrate my heart before I had to keep going and tackle dinner and baths and bedtime.

Just then, I heard the quiet voice of my young daughter say, "Jesus, help Mommy. Amen." Without prompting, she had reminded me of His presence and extended His love through her small arms. Sometimes God speaks to us in ways that we expect and at other times in unexpected voices, like the small voice of a child.

In 1 Kings, chapter 19, we can read about a radical encounter Elijah experienced with the Lord. The people of Israel had turned from following God and were worshipping a false god named Baal.

To turn the hearts of the people back to the Lord, Elijah offered a challenge. He called all the prophets of Baal together and told them to try to call down fire to consume their sacrifice. The false prophets were unable to do it, but Elijah turned and told men to pour water all over his sacrifice, and then in a loud voice called out to God, "'LORD, the God of Abraham, Isaac and Israel, let it be known today that you are God in Israel.' . . .

"Then the fire of the LORD fell and burned up the sacrifice, the wood, the stones and the soil, and also licked up the water in the trench."[50]

The Israelites began to worship the Lord, and Elijah had all the false prophets of Baal killed. When the king's wife, a worshipper of Baal, heard what Elijah had done, she promised to have Elijah killed in retaliation.

Rather than trust the Lord to prove Himself mighty again, Elijah ran for his life to the same mountain where God had spoken to Moses. To Moses, God had spoken in fire and smoke and a thunderous voice. But when Elijah arrived, the Lord prompted him, saying,

"'Go out and stand on the mountain in the presence of the LORD, for the LORD is about to pass by.'

"Then a great and powerful wind tore the mountains apart and shattered the rocks before the LORD, but the LORD was not in the wind. After the wind there was an earthquake, but the LORD was not in the earthquake. After the earthquake came a fire, but the LORD was not in the fire. And after the fire came a gentle whisper. When Elijah heard it, he pulled his cloak over his face and went out and stood at the mouth of the cave."[51]

Sometimes we are looking for God to speak to us in the way He has spoken to us and to others in the past, and He surprises us. We might be listening for His message about a certain situation in our lives to come from the booming voice on a church platform, and we might instead find His counsel through an unexpected word of a trusted friend. Or we might turn to a friend and instead find God's message delivered through encouragement from a stranger. God might use a perfectly timed text, a song on the radio, or a post online. God might even speak to us through the whispered words of our children. The key to hearing God is knowing first what He sounds like through His Word and then paying attention to hear His leading even in unexpected places.

When the world says, "Your God is limited," we hear Him saying, *I am not restricted in the ways that I speak to My children. I know there are ways you want Me to reveal My Truth to you. I know you prefer that I always spoke in a loud, clear voice, but sometimes I call to you in a whisper. I speak to you in a way that makes you lean into Me and pay attention to Me in a new way. My voice always draws you closer.*

When the voice of the Lord doesn't seem to be coming the way we expected, we should listen and wait. He just might surprise us.

Lord, teach us to pay attention to those around us in such a way that we don't miss Your words in theirs. Teach us to appreciate the whisper of the Holy Spirit to our hearts as it draws us to You in a new way. In Jesus's name we pray. Amen.

Don't Curse What I Said to Bless

God Speaks Through Balaam's Donkey

Numbers 22

---

*T*his will never get any better. This is just the way it is, and I might as well accept it. What is the matter with them? They're just strong willed, and they always will be. They're just bad listeners. He's never going to help me with the kids. This is too hard.

Raise your hand if you have ever had even one of those thoughts slip from your lips. Okay, so you don't actually have to raise your hand, but let's do something and bravely admit that we don't always say what we know to be true about our families.

In the middle of a disagreement with my husband or at the end of a long day with my kids, sometimes my mouth says what I'm feeling rather than what God says is true. Sometimes my feelings are liars. I don't mean that what I'm experiencing isn't real. My experiences are real, but the feelings that come from my experiences do not always reveal God's Truth. And sometimes my feelings cause my mouth to curse what God says to bless.

There is a story found in Numbers 22 about a wicked prophet named Balaam who attempted to curse what God said to bless. Balaam was a prophet who heard from the Lord and spoke on behalf of the Lord, but he was also corrupt and persuaded by personal gain. An evil king named Balak wanted Balaam to speak on behalf of God and curse God's people so that he could conquer them. When the evil king sent for the corrupt prophet, God said, "Since these men have come to summon you, go with them, but do only what I tell you."[52]

However, God knew this prophet's true motives, and the angel of the Lord met him on the road with a sword drawn to oppose him. The problem was that only this prophet's donkey could see the angel. When the donkey continued to veer from the course, Balaam beat the donkey.

"The LORD opened the donkey's mouth, and it said to Balaam, 'What have I done to you to make you beat me these three times?' . . .

"Then the LORD opened Balaam's eyes, and he saw the angel of the LORD standing in the road with his sword drawn. So he bowed low and fell face-down. . . . Then the LORD said again, 'Go with the men, but speak only what I tell you.' "[53]

So Balaam went with the king's officials. When it came time to make a declaration over God's people, Balaam said, "How can I curse those whom God has not cursed?"[54] And he offered a blessing.

What does this story have to do with us? We might not be wicked prophets (praise the Lord), but rather than declare what our hearts know to be true over our families, we let discouragement and hopelessness slip from our lips. We let our corrupt feelings persuade us to say things we don't really believe are true.

When we feel as though everything is hopeless, we shouldn't agree with that emotion. We should acknowledge how we feel and then say, "God, You are our hope in every situation." When we think things are always going to be this hard or just as they are right now, we should recognize it as a lie and agree with Truth responding, "Lord, Your mercies are new every morning, and it won't always be like this." When we're convinced our kids are always going to act a certain way, we should say, "Lord, help them become better listeners (or kind or obedient)."

I'm not asking us to redefine our realities. There's often a reason we feel the way we do. I'm asking us to decide that our mouths will partner with Truth and declare what we really believe.

I think the Lord would remind you and me using words He spoke to Balaam: *Say only what I tell you to say. Make declarations over your family based on what I say is true. Use the power of your voice to speak life and not death. Because it will get better, it won't always be this way, and your Father in heaven is working all things out for the good of those who love Him and are called according to His purposes.*[55] *Remind your family and your feelings this week that you know who is in control, and then hand both over to Me.*

Lord, we respond to You by saying we are sorry. We are sorry for the times we agreed with the voice of discouragement rather than the voice of our Father. We will bless our families. We won't let our feelings cause us to curse what You say to bless. In Jesus's name we pray. Amen.

Celebrate with Them

God Speaks to Jonah

Jonah

Bless the Lord, my children have reached the age where they can help with chores. And I love to let them help! They're past the stage where helping means making a bigger mess, and my eight- and seven-year-olds have reached the point where they can unload the dishwasher or vacuum on their own. But their three-year-old little brother, still has a hard time completing the big-kid jobs.

One afternoon, they were each assigned their own age-appropriate tasks, and I even told them that I'd pay them a little for their hard work. My youngest finished first.

When they had all finished, I passed out the same amount of money to each of them. "No fair! Why does Jaxton get the same amount as we do! His work wasn't nearly as hard!"

I did my best to explain that it wasn't hard to them because they were older, but to Jaxton it had been real work. They didn't care for my explanation. They saw money coming to their little brother easily, and they considered it unfair.

I can't say their feelings were lost on me. I have experienced something similar when I've seen a friend achieve with ease what doesn't come naturally for me. Have you ever had this happen to you?

Perhaps you struggled to become pregnant and you had a friend who got pregnant in her first month of trying. Maybe you worked and worked for a promotion, only to have someone who had been with the company for less time show up and take the job. Maybe you've been trying to get your kids to sleep through the night for the last three years and you have a friend with a two-month-old who is getting eight hours of sleep a night.

I have to be honest, I struggle in situations like these. *God, why are You making it so easy on them? Why isn't it harder for her? Do you remember what I had to go through when all they had to do was _____?*

In the story of Jonah, we find that he struggled just as much as I do sometimes. If you remember, God told Jonah to warn the people of Nineveh of God's coming judgment. Jonah didn't want to go and tried to run away, but he ended up on a boat in the middle of a storm and the only way to stop the storm and save the lives of the other men on the boat was to be thrown into the water.

Poor Jonah goes into the water, the storm stops, the men on the boat marvel, and Jonah is swallowed by a fish big enough to keep him alive for three days before spitting him onto the shore just so he can finally go where the Lord called him in the first place . . . Nineveh.

When Jonah finally made it to the city, he spent days walking around telling the people, "Forty more days and Nineveh will be overthrown."[56]

Jonah believed God would do this, as did the Ninevites. A fast was declared, and "when God saw what they did and how they turned from their evil ways, he relented and did not bring on them the destruction he had threatened."[57]

But this made Jonah angry. He said to the Lord, "Isn't this what I said, Lord, when I was still at home? . . . I knew that you are a gracious and compassionate God, slow to anger and abounding in love, a God who relents from sending calamity. Now, LORD, take away my life, for it is better for me to die than to live."[58]

Whoa, Jonah. That seems a little extreme. But to Jonah, God's mercy didn't seem fair. *These people just get to go free, and I had to be thrown into the sea, swallowed by a fish, and thrown up on the shore?*

"But the LORD replied, 'Is it right for you to be angry?'"[59]

I think sometimes we need the same reminder. We need to hear the Lord compassionately whispering to us, *Is it right for you to be angry at the way I take care of others? Is it right for you to want them to experience trials because you did or to wish life was just a little bit harder for them so that you weren't alone in your suffering? Don't you see that I am a good Father who takes care of all my children? Don't you see that I desire to take care of you in ways they won't understand either? Instead of wishing it was harder for them, celebrate! Celebrate because you have seen Me do it for them, and you can trust that I am working your life out for your good as well. Allow me to remove the bitterness so that you can taste and see that I'm good and not just to you but to those you love as well.*

We might not always understand the justice and mercy of God, but when we adjust our thinking from fairness to goodness, we will see that God is equally good to all those He loves.

Lord, help us not become angry or bitter toward others You love, but help us see that You are good toward all Your children. Remove a heart of frustration, and help us celebrate every good victory in the lives of those we love. In Jesus's name. Amen.

You, the Incredible Mom!

God Commissions Gideon

Judges 6

"Brave and strong woman, incredible mother, mighty warrior of God!" Can you imagine if an angel of the Lord appeared to you in your baby's nursery as you cried your way through a middle-of-the-night diaper change? What if an angel appeared to you in the car-rider pickup line at school and said that? What if an angel showed up and said those words right after you had a hard conversation with your preteen about boundaries? What if the Lord Himself showed up and said those words to you right now?

If you're anything like me, you might look around and say, "Me? Brave . . . strong . . . incredible?" But this is exactly what the Lord says to both of us right now. He looks at us and He calls us by what He already knows to be true about us. He sees within us the very best version of us and addresses us by it. How do I know this is true?

One of my favorite stories in Scripture is the story of Gideon leading the Israelites in their defeat of the Midianites. The Israelites had turned away from God, and they had begun to worship false gods. As a result, the Lord did not protect the Israelites when the Midianites oppressed them, but God had a plan to rescue the Israelites. He would use Gideon.

Gideon was threshing wheat in a winepress to keep the Midianites from finding it when an angel of the Lord appeared and sat under a tree nearby. The angel called out to Gideon, "The LORD is with you, mighty warrior."[60]

Gideon had a quick reply, but I wonder if there was a split second where he looked around the winepress and thought, "Mighty . . . warrior? Sure you got the right guy? You do see that I'm hiding, right?" But in that moment, the Lord called out in Gideon what he would go on to become with His help. The Lord led him and only three hundred men in defeating one of the largest armies that had ever come against the Israelites. Gideon became a mighty warrior who had the Lord with him, but I bet those words didn't make much sense to him when he was hiding from the Midianites in a winepress.

Notice the Lord didn't call out to Gideon, "Cowardly pagan worshipper, the Lord wants to use you if you'll change." Nope. God called him a mighty warrior because the Lord saw what Gideon would accomplish as though it had already happened. He does the same for us. He calls us by what He knows we will become and not just what we think we are. He doesn't call out to us, "Pathetic excuse for a mom," "Joke of a wife," or "Ridiculous fraud and failure." He looks at us and doesn't see any of the things we often fear we are or will become. No, friend. He looks at us and says, *Beloved daughter, warrior woman, blessed by her children, loved by her husband, fully able, more than a conqueror, incredible mother! I am with you! You are going to get through this! I know because I've already seen you do it! You're going to figure it out! I know because I know how I'm going to lead you. You're the best mom for these kids! You're just the right choice for this work! I see who you really are!*

What would our lives be like if we retrained ourselves to see what the Lord sees when He looks at us? What kind of mom or wife or friend would we become if we believed that what God knows to be true of us is actually true? You might feel far from brave. You might feel far from full of love and joy and hope. You might feel like the worst mom in the world, but the Lord knows every one of your incredible moments, and those are the ones that He uses to identify you.

Lord, we have spent so many years of our lives focused on all our failures that they feel like adequate titles. But, God, when You look at us, You only see Your daughters, fully deserving of love. Help us to retrain our hearts to see ourselves from Your perspective. In Jesus's name we pray. Amen.

I Will Accomplish My Plan Through You

God Sends a Message to Mary

Luke 1

One of the things I worry about the most is whether I'm going to make the right choices for my family. I'm afraid that if I make the wrong choice, I'll mess something up and ruin my kids forever. That fear seems kind of dramatic to say out loud, I'm likely not the only mom who worries about the weight of her decisions. The pressure to make the right choice can be overwhelming.

Starting from the beginning, as parents we decide everything from where our kids will sleep, what they will eat, and how we will diaper them and help them soothe. The decision-making continues into schooling and friends and how we will parent. The choices we make grow as our children grow and seem to become more and more important. This can create a huge mental load. We feel especially burdened by the responsibilities when it feels as though we are shouldering them alone, even if we are married.

But see, this fear is actually rooted in lies. The Enemy wants us to believe that if we make the wrong choices our kids will suffer, and he wants us to believe that we are the only ones carrying the responsibility of each choice. But God is intimately involved in everything we do. When we gave our lives over to Him, His Holy Spirit came to live in our hearts and began offering the directions for each step. The Word says in Psalm 37:23 (KJV), "The steps of a good man are ordered by the LORD." This includes our mothering.

Additionally, God is going to accomplish His purposes in our lives and in the lives of our children no matter how the Enemy tries to thwart it. We're afraid that if we make the wrong choice, the ultimate plan of God is going to be stopped somehow. But the Enemy has never been able to stop God from accomplishing what He wants to accomplish. If God wants it to happen, it will happen.

Just think of Mary, Jesus's mother. The angel said to her, "The Holy Spirit will come on you, and the power of the Most High will overshadow you. So the holy one to be born will be called the Son of God."[61] Mary was a virgin. She wasn't even married, and yet God accomplished His purpose to bring Jesus into the world through her.

The woman who carried the Son of God within her only had to submit to God's plan. She didn't have to do anything but respond to the angel, " 'I am the Lord's servant,' Mary answered. 'May it happen to me according to your word.' "[62] The fulfillment of God's plans through her rested on His provision and His wisdom and His careful strategy—and on her willingness to be used. The baby came no matter what.

While we aren't carrying the Son of God within us in human form, we are carrying the promise of His Holy Spirit inside us. And we have the opportunity to respond to the Lord, knowing that God will accomplish His purposes through us if we are simply willing to say, "Yes. Lead me and use me, Lord."

God is going to accomplish in our families what He wants to accomplish, and we don't need to fear that we are solely responsible for making it happen. He is faithful to order our steps. He is faithful to fill us with His wisdom. He is faithful to guide and direct us. God wants us to succeed, and He wants our families to thrive.

So that lie that says you're on your own and if you make a mistake you are going to ruin your kids is simply trying to distract us from the powerful Truth that God says over us: *I am within you. I will not fail you or forsake you. Give me the weight of the responsibility that you have tried to shoulder alone. It is My plan for your family, and you are a vessel I use to accomplish it. So as long as you are willing to be used by My Holy Spirit and to follow His lead, then you don't need to worry that you alone are making the decisions.*

Remember this. You might not have an angel standing in front of you, telling you what's coming next the way Mary did, but you have the Holy Spirit who lives within you. And as you come to know His voice, and trust Him to lead you, you will realize that He was involved in all those decisions you thought you were making on your own. The baby is coming no matter what. Your job is to repeat Mary's response: "I am willing to be used of the Lord. Let it happen to me as you have said."

Lord, let it happen as You have already seen in Your heart. You have trusted us with these kids. You have trusted us with the lives we've been given, and we don't carry the weight of seeing Your plans accomplished alone. We give back to You what we have tried to carry, and we remember that You are in control. In Jesus's name we pray. Amen.

Trust My Perspective

God Sends a Message to Joseph

Matthew 2

---

*I*t was early spring and one of the first major tornadoes of the season was barreling down I-40 with a projected line of impact passing directly over my parents' house. While the weather forecasters in Oklahoma do a fantastic job of providing real-time information about where the storms are and where they are headed, the power had gone out, and my parents didn't have access to the TV or a live weather map.

We had been keeping up with storms all afternoon, so it wasn't a surprise when my parents called and said, "We don't know what to do. The storm is coming, and we don't have a storm shelter." Forecasters were calling this tornado an F5, which meant a possibility of winds more than 260 miles per hour. An interior room or a closet could not be expected to provide safety. Without a belowground shelter, they were in grave danger. They had to leave.

This is something that most Oklahomans know not to do. We are advised to never try to outrun the storm. You are supposed to find the closest safe shelter and wait for it to pass. But on this May day, that was not an option. If the storm remained on track, my parents likely would not have survived if they had stayed, and if they made the wrong turn, their lives would also be in danger.

It was probably one of the scariest moments of my life, knowing that I was an hour and a half away and couldn't help them except to be their eyes, watching the storm on my TV and helping them decide which way they needed to go to avoid it. I began to pray, *Lord, show me which way to have them go. Stop the storm. Calm the winds. Help my parents.* I was so scared, but the Lord was leading all of us that day.

They ended up at a public shelter in a nearby town, while the storm turned south just five miles from their home—the direction they would have likely gone if I hadn't been watching and guiding them.

Sometimes God stands up and calms the storm, and sometimes to save us, He helps us move out of its path. This is exactly the method that God used to save Joseph and his young family.

Shortly after the wise men arrived with their gifts for Jesus, an angel appeared to Joseph in a dream and gave him a message from the Lord, "Get up, . . . take the child and his mother and escape to Egypt. Stay there until I tell you, for Herod is going to search for the child to kill him."[63] So they left during the night, and they stayed in Egypt until Herod died and the threat to Jesus's life had passed.

Would it have been more convenient for this young family if the Lord had simply withheld the threat? Absolutely. But sometimes God removes us from the threat instead. He saves us by removing us from what would harm us.

I've had plenty of moments in my life when I wondered why God was asking me to leave or stop or move from one assignment to the next. I've had plenty of moments when God has said, "It's time to go," and we've gone. Sometimes we know there is a particular situation that we need to leave, and other times we are simply trusting the guidance of the Holy Spirit to know best even when things look okay to us.

But we trust the Lord, because He can see what we can't. He gently reminds our hearts, *I have access to the map. I can see all aspects of every circumstance. I have heaven's perspective, and I am the only One who can move your family in My timing as I see fit. So follow Me quickly. Don't delay. Don't doubt. Don't wonder if I know best. Do what I say and go. You can trust that My path is the safest to your future.*

I don't know what He's asking you to leave. I don't know what He has removed you from in the past. But I know that He is leading us because He loves us and He can see what we can't. That is something we can fully trust today.

Lord, thank You for removing us from what would harm us. Thank You for taking us out of the path of danger. When we don't see what's coming, You do. Help us to trust You continually and listen carefully. In Jesus's name. Amen.

There Is Purpose to This Work

Jesus Tells John to Baptize Him

Matthew 3

I was sorting through my closet, grabbing the free hangers so I could put away a load of clothes, and all I could think about was all the much more important things I needed to be doing instead. As a matter of fact, I was thinking about how I needed to sit down at my desk and work on this book.

Hanging up clothes was not how I wanted to be spending my time.

That's when I saw the faces of our friends serving in Costa Rica. I am not sure why the Holy Spirit chose to get His message across this way, but one second I was picking up hangers and thinking about the "more important" things I needed to be doing, and the next I was thinking of the mission work my husband had completed a few years before in the jungle.

As if watching a slideshow, I remembered the photos and videos Jared shared when he returned. I saw the work of his team. I saw ordinary moments—cooking meals and playing with the locals. I saw ordinary and yet extraordinary work being done for the kingdom through relationship and service.

And in an instant, I realized that if I had been doing the same basic task for any other family, I would have considered it an act of love. If I had been helping a woman clean clothes for her family on the mission field, I would have seen it as a way to expand the kingdom by communicating God's love for her and her family. But because I was doing it for my own family, it felt like a distraction from the *more important* work.

I know that motherhood requires us to serve in ways that often feel monotonous, that often don't seem to be of much eternal value. But you know, I think every single thing we do for our families has the potential to be an extension of God's love. I think we have the same capability to reveal the heart of the Father to care for His children each time we take care of even the most basic needs of those given to us. We might just need the Lord to remind us that we don't always understand the value of what we are doing.

Matthew 3 records the story of Jesus's baptism. His cousin, John, had been baptizing believers into repentance, calling them to prepare their hearts for the coming Messiah who would baptize with the Holy Spirit and fire. When John saw Jesus coming to be baptized, he said, "'I need to be baptized by you, and do you come to me?'

"Jesus replied, 'Let it be so now; it is proper for us to do this to fulfill all righteousness.' Then John consented," and Jesus was baptized.[64]

Scripture says that at the moment Jesus came out of the water, "heaven was opened, and he saw the Spirit of God descending like a dove and alighting on him. And a voice from heaven said, 'This is my Son, whom I love; with him I am well pleased.'"[65]

There were many people, including John, who questioned why Jesus had to be baptized as a sign of repentance if Jesus was sinless. The truth is, Jesus was baptized by John because it was all part of God's plan for humanity's redemption, even if it didn't make sense to anyone else. It had eternal value, but it was hard to see from earth's perspective.

I think sometimes we are a lot like John, with hearts that fail to see the eternal value in what Jesus asks us to do. I believe the Lord would remind each of us, *There is purpose to this work. There is value in each act of love you show to those I've placed in your care. I can see the eternal impact. So don't despise the simple things. Don't deny the opportunity to reveal My heart to those I've given to you to love on My behalf. You might not be able to understand, but this mission of motherhood will grow My kingdom. This is important work.*

Lord, show us how to love our families well. Shift our perspectives, so we don't despise moments of exhausting sacrifice but see them instead as heaven's heartbeat. We want to see our service to our families as You see it. In Jesus's name we pray. Amen.

I Am So Proud of You

God Speaks at Jesus's Baptism

Matthew 3

When I was little, my parents would write notes on yellow lined paper and tuck them into my lunch box. Every day, I would open my lunch and hope my note said, "Surprise! We're checking you out of school early today. See you in an hour!" But it never did. Instead, those notes were filled with encouragement: "You're the best!" "Hope you're having the very best day, because you deserve it!" "You can do anything!" "I love you so much!" "I'm so proud of you!"

While they might not have disclosed surprise early checkouts, I still saved each one. And as an adult looking back, I can't think of anything better than a container full of my parents' affirmations. What a gift it is for a child to know that she is loved and accepted, safe and secure, just as she is.

Before Jesus entered into full-time ministry, before He healed the sick or cast out demons or called His disciples, He was baptized by His cousin, John. When Jesus came up out of the water, "a voice from heaven said, 'This is my Son, whom I love; with Him I am well pleased.'"[66] He had the approval of His heavenly Father, who said, "This is My Boy! I'm proud of Him! I love Him!" Our Father loves us the same way and is just as proud, which is important for us to know! It's important that we store up His affirmations in our hearts.

It can be difficult to hear Him say how proud He is of us when we're so busy listening to the Enemy tell us that we're terrible failures. The truth is, our Enemy is terrified that we're going to remember that we carry inside ourselves the same power that enabled Jesus to rise from the grave. Or that we are going to remember that when God looks at us, He sees His Son and says, "I am well pleased." So our Enemy spends his days trying to get us to believe we're nothing.

But what would happen if we remembered who we are? What if we looked in the mirror and saw the fire that Jesus sees when He looks at us? What if instead of paying attention to the voice of the Enemy, we heard the Father saying, *I'm so proud of you. I love you. You're the greatest! I want today to be the best day for you!* How would His affirmation impact how we are able to love our families?

There's too much love waiting to be poured out by God through us for us to waste one more minute believing God's not proud of us. Our kids desperately need their parents to be confident of God's love and approval so they willingly pass it out to them. Our kids need us to see each opportunity to extend the same type of affirmation to them. There is no greater gift we can offer our children than our love, blessing, and public affirmation of who they are as well.

Let's shake hell up today. Let's love like crazy. Let's give ourselves and our families grace. Jesus died for this. So let's live like it. Repeat heaven's words over yourself right now. "This is my daughter. I am so proud of her!"

Lord, we don't want to listen to the lies of the Enemy anymore. We want to hear Your voice, as if it is a note tucked into our day, telling us that we are loved and accepted, safe and secure in You. In Jesus's name we pray. Amen.

The Enemy Has No Authority over You

Jesus Speaks to Satan

Matthew 4

I was standing at the kitchen sink, taking care of the last of the dinner dishes from the night before, and I was proud of myself. Please understand, I'm not normally proud of myself for doing dishes. But on this morning, I really didn't feel like taking care of them. I really wanted to pretend there wasn't twenty minutes' worth of rinsing required before I could even load the dishwasher.

But rather than ignore what had to be done, I jumped in and just tackled it. I was in one of those moods where you find yourself congratulating yourself on doing something that should probably just come naturally. I was scrubbing noodles dried onto pans and thinking, *Today is going to be a good day. I can totally take on today. I'm strong. I'm victorious.* I was just washing dishes, but I was pretty sure I could do just about anything.

Then I heard that little lying whisper, *No. Today, is going to be like every other day, and you'll be frustrated and exhausted by noon.*

That thought stopped me. *Wait. That's not the voice of my Father,* I thought.

I know what my Dad sounds like, and that's not it. That discouragement came straight from the depths of hell.

In the process of tuning my heart to the voice of the Lord, I have become keenly aware of what God says and what He doesn't say in His Word. And He doesn't say, "You're going to be exhausted and frustrated." No. He says, "Peace I leave with you. . . . Do not let your heart be troubled."[67]

The truth is, sometimes I let these little discouraging thoughts slip by. I just brush them off and let them go, forgetting that they have a source who needs to be silenced.

Fortunately, Jesus taught us how to rebuke our Enemy. When Jesus was in the wilderness, the Enemy came to Him and spoke to Him as well. Satan knew the Truth, but desperate to have Jesus give over His authority, the Enemy twisted Scripture as he quoted it:

"'If you are the Son of God, tell these stones to become bread.'

"Jesus answered, 'It is written: "Man shall not live on bread alone, but on every word that comes from the mouth of God."'"[68] Again and again, Jesus reminded the Enemy of the complete Truth, until finally, Jesus said to him, "Away from me, Satan! For it is written: 'Worship the Lord your God, and serve him only.'"[69]

Friend, there are times we let discouraging or shameful or guilt-filled thoughts go as if we came up with them on our own. But that's exactly what our Enemy wants us to do. He wants us to just pretend he doesn't exist. When we think thoughts that do not align with the Truth that God reveals in His Word, we need to remember their source and silence them. We need to hear the Lord reminding us to "demolish arguments and every pretension that sets itself up against the knowledge of God, and . . . take captive every thought to make it obedient to Christ."[70]

We know the voice of the Lord, and we know that He has zero tolerance for the lies of the Enemy. And no matter what the Enemy would try to have you believe, your Father in heaven is speaking His loving Truth over your heart. He's reminding you that you don't have to put up with the tormenting thoughts of the Enemy. And I hear Him saying to us right now, *When the Enemy comes to steal your peace, destroy your hope, and kill your dreams, tell him to go away. Tell him that you live on every word that comes from the heart of God. Tell him that you are Mine. And tell him that he has no authority over you.*

Let's stay vigilant, friends. Not just for ourselves, but for the sake of our families relying on us to relay powerful Truth.

Lord, we don't want to let thoughts from the Enemy linger. We don't want to give his voice any room in our hearts. As we tune our hearts to Your voice, create an intolerance for anything that would desire to discourage or shame us. In Jesus's name we pray. Amen.

I Know What You'll Do Next

Jesus Invites Peter to Follow Him

Luke 5

I dropped into the chair in my new sunny California office. *How did we get here, God? What do we do next? And what do I do about* _____, _____, *and* _____? That deep exhaustion turned into a silent cry. And with tears running down my face, I heard the Lord whisper to my heart, *"What lies are you believing right now that are causing you to feel afraid and discouraged?"*

It was one of those Dad questions. You know, the kind of questions a parent asks his child when he already knows the answer and just wants his kid to come up with it on her own.

Let me be clear. This wasn't what I wanted God to say in this moment. I wanted Him to tell me what to do next. I wanted Him to map out my next three steps so I could know that He had a plan in place.

What lies am I believing?

I could identify them. That was easy. I knew how I felt, but I also knew the Truth. It felt like the answers would never come. It felt like it was all up to me to figure it out on my own. I felt stuck and yet required to know the right next step. But I also knew in my heart that the answers would come and the Lord was continuing to lead me.

So then the Lord asked kindly, *Do you trust Me?*

In that moment, God wasn't giving me answers that would bring me peace. He was teaching me how to have peace even when it's not time to know the answers. He was teaching me that, to stop feeling discouraged, I just had to decide that I could trust Him until the answers came. This is the same invitation that the Lord extended to some of the first disciples.

When Jesus called His first disciples, they were on a boat. The crowd had been pressing against Him, so He climbed on a boat and told the fishermen to push away from the shore. He spoke to the crowd, and when He was done, Jesus told the fishermen to let down their nets. They had been fishing all night and hadn't caught anything, but a man named Peter answered Jesus, "Master, we've worked hard all night and haven't caught anything. But because you say so, I will let down the nets."[71]

They let the nets down and immediately caught so many fish that their nets began to break. When Peter saw this, he fell at Jesus's knees, but Jesus answered Peter, "Don't be afraid; from now on you will fish for people."[72]

Without a plan. Without a full layout of the next couple of steps or the next few years. Without anything but the offer, Peter left his boats and chose to trust the Lord. He left behind the life he had known and set out on a new adventure of faith.

We are presented with the same question. Just as Jesus asked that day on the water and that afternoon in my office—and even in this moment as you read these words—God asks us again and again, *Will you trust Me even when I don't tell you fully what's coming next? Will you hold on to Me, remembering that I am peace? There is security in answers, but there is more security in the One who* holds all the answers. If you have Me then you have everything you need. Don't be afraid. I know what you'll do next.

Lord, even without a clear path, we trust You, knowing You see clearly. We say that we will follow and we will trust, and we thank You for the chance to do both. In Jesus's name we pray. Amen.

I Knew You Before I Called You

Jesus Calls Nathanael

John 1

As we pulled up to our house in northwest Oklahoma with our newborn baby girl, there was a tornado about ten miles south of town that we could see from my front porch. You'd think that I might be terrified. You'd think that I would at least be just a little bit concerned. But really, the tornado didn't even faze me. I have proof because my husband filmed the whole thing.

I was so focused on the fact that I was now the mom of a sixteen-month-old and a newborn, that an actual tornado within just a few miles of my house was the least of my worries. How was I supposed to take care of two babies? How?

I wish that I could tell you it was a breeze. I wish I could tell you that just like the storm outside, the storm inside me calmed and everything was fine. But I can't. Being the mom of two very small children felt impossible some days.

But I remember one particular afternoon, not too long after, I looked around and thought, *Wow. Everyone is still alive, and I got to shower today. Maybe I can do this.*

And the Lord gently reminded me again and again, *I knew you could.*

On the days I wasn't sure, God was. On the days I wasn't confident that God had made the right choice giving these kids to me, He was confident.

Because He knew me long before He called me to motherhood. Long before He put the dream in my heart, He knew exactly what would be required of me. And He knew that together, we could do it. This is true for the call of God into any area of life. God knows us before He calls us. We see this in Nathanael's story in Scripture.

In John 1 we find the story about Jesus calling some of His disciples to follow Him for the first time. When Jesus invited Philip, Philip couldn't keep it to himself. Thrilled to have found the promised Messiah, he ran to find his friend Nathanael.

While the two men, Philip and Nathanael, were still walking toward him, Jesus said about Nathanael, "Now here is a genuine son of Israel—a man of complete integrity."[73]

Nathanael was shocked and said, "But you've never met me. How do you know me?"

Jesus answered, "I saw you while you were still under the fig tree before Philip called you."

At this response, Nathanael said, "You are the Son of God."[74]

Oh, if we could just wrap our arms around this Truth in our own lives. "Before you even heard about Me, I saw you."

We know that God sees us even when it seems as though we are all alone. We know that God doesn't miss any detail of our lives. But from this passage, we can also confidently declare that before Jesus called us to follow Him, He knew our hearts and our character.

Jesus looked right at Nathanael and revealed the type of man he was. God knows us just as personally. He knew who we were before He called us to motherhood, and He made the decision to invite us on this journey anyway. He didn't call us to be mothers to watch us fail. He called us to be mothers because He saw deep within us the strength it would take to succeed.

Where fear might distract us from the truth, where doubt might taunt that we will never be enough for our children, God says, *A mighty daughter, fully capable, full of hope and strength. I have known that you have what it takes to be who I've called you to be since before you were even born. Don't rely on your own strength. Ask Me to help you. It's My calling. It's your destiny. And it's our journey. I knew you could do it, because we will be doing it together.*

Lord, thank You for seeing within us what we don't see. Thank You for calling out the good in us so that we are able to hear what You think of us. Help us rely on Your strength. In Jesus's name we pray. Amen.

I'm Inviting You to Be Part of the Miracle

Jesus Speaks to the Wedding Servants

John 2

I'm guilty of wanting the Lord to intervene in my situation so long as I don't have to do anything scary as part of the process. For example, I'm fully willing to trust that the Lord wants to supernaturally provide for my family's financial needs, provided He doesn't ask me to give away a large chunk of the last of our finances to someone else. Or, I'm fully prepared to pray and wait on the Lord to intervene with that friend who doesn't know Him, but don't make me call that person and address some past hurt or offense that He says we need to sort through. Or how about this? "I'm willing to bring the gospel to the world; I'll even start a Bible study at my house, God, but don't make me go talk to that stranger at the grocery store because that sounds super hard and awkward today."

Don't get me wrong. I've done all these things. I've given away the last of the money in the account because I felt the Lord telling me I should, and He did come through in a supernatural way and provide for our family. I did reach out for reconciliation with a loved one. I did stop and talk to the stranger in the grocery store. I have done all these things, but if I'm being completely honest, I would much rather my contribution of faith be something so much easier—like just believing God will do it.

Often the Lord invites us to be a part of the process. And when He does, it's important that we do exactly as He directs, without cutting corners or making any substitutions for His specific instructions. We see how important details are in the story of Jesus's first recorded miracle at a wedding at Cana in Galilee.

> When the wine ran out, Jesus's mother came to Him and said, "They have no more wine."
>
> "Woman, why do you involve me?" Jesus replied. "My hour has not yet come."
>
> His mother said to the servants, "Do whatever he tells you."
>
> Nearby stood six stone water jars, the kind used by the Jews for ceremonial washing, each holding from twenty to thirty gallons.
>
> Jesus said to the servants, "Fill the jars with water"; so they filled them to the brim.
>
> Then he told them, "Now draw some out and take it to the master of the banquet."
>
> They did so, and the master of the banquet tasted the water that had been turned into wine. He did not realize where the wine had come from, though the servants who had drawn the water knew.[75]

Scripture says that when Jesus told the servants to fill the jars, they filled them to the brim. I wonder where they had to go to get that water and how far they had to carry it. But I love imagining these servants carefully doing exactly as Jesus had instructed. He didn't have some track record of miracles. He was just Mary's son, yet for whatever reason, the servants filled the jars to the very top.

And Scripture says that when they took the wine to the master of the wedding, he didn't know where it had come from, but the servants who had been a part of the process knew. Everyone got to enjoy the result of the miracle, but only the servants fully knew what Jesus had done that night.

In our lives, it would be great if God would just manifest the things that we are asking Him for. It would have been great if Jesus could have just dipped His finger into each of the jars and turned the water already there into wine.

But He invited the servants to be a part of the process, and when He did, He gave them the chance to be a part of something few other people in attendance would even believe.

I think each of us can admit there are times in our lives when the work God calls us to feels exhausting, repetitive, and ridiculous. *What am I doing this for, God? Can't You just accomplish Your purposes another way? Can't You bring the provision or healing or forgiveness or reconciliation, or increase of faith some other way, God?* But He graciously says to each of us, *Fill the jars. Do exactly as I say. Even if it feels silly or you don't understand. Even if it's repetitive or it's outside your normal scope of work. Even if you didn't sign up for this or you don't see how it's going to work out. I'm going to come through for you, but I'm inviting you to be a part of the miracle.*

Lord, help us become those who do exactly as You say, because You were the One who said it. Lord, we commit to doing as You direct, even if it is repetitive or out of our comfort zone. We want to be a part of the miracle. In Jesus's name we pray. Amen.

I Will Come Help You

Jesus Speaks to the Roman Centurion

Matthew 8

All three of my children had a miserable flu virus recently. They were running high fevers and coughing, and they had severe aches and chills. Kids always require so much extra attention and love while they're sick. I have the privilege of being their mom and the one who got to do this loving, but it came with so much extra responsibility. As a mom with only two hands, it was hard to make sure my kids had what they needed night and day. I was so tired. Beyond tired. To my bones exhausted from taking care of them.

My husband was working out of town one night, and I was trying to get all three kids comfortable in their beds. My daughter wanted me to stay with her as she shook from her fever, and my youngest son was struggling to quit coughing. I needed to get a breathing treatment started for him, and I needed be with my other children at the exact same time. I felt like I was going to break under the pressure of who needed me most and the anxiety of not being enough for any of them. At that moment, I prayed aloud, "Lord, I need You to come and sit here on Kadence's bed with her while I take care of Jaxton. I need You to be in this room right now with her so she doesn't feel alone. Help her sense Your presence, God. Hold her close while I have to be out of the room."

I had never prayed a prayer like that aloud in the presence of my kids. I didn't think it through, actually. I just decided to ask God for the help I knew He could provide. I asked God to come and help me parent my children.

Immediately, both Kadence and I felt at peace. She settled into her bed, able to rest at the thought of Jesus sitting there beside her, holding her hand and not leaving her alone. And I was able to leave her to help Jaxton, because I knew that she wasn't alone.

We often forget that Jesus wants to help us parent our kids. He wants us to come to Him with everything, trusting that it is His good desire to intervene in every area our lives.

There's a story found in Matthew about a Roman Centurion coming to Jesus and asking Him to heal his servant.

Jesus said to him, "I will come and heal him."

The Centurion answered and said, "Lord, I am not worthy that You should come under my roof. But only speak a word, and my servant will be healed." . . .

When Jesus heard it, He marveled, and said to those who followed, "Assuredly, I say to you, I have not found such great faith, not even in Israel!" . . . Then Jesus said to the centurion, "Go your way; and as you have believed, so let it be done for you." And his servant was healed that same hour."[76]

Often, we look at this story as a showcase of this man's faith in Jesus: "Just send your word and my servant will be healed." It is remarkable that this man didn't require the Lord to go but trusted in the power of God's spoken word to heal his servant. But I want to point out something else in this story. I want us to see how Jesus willingly offered to go with this man.

In our lives we often overlook the willingness of God to intervene on our behalf. We overlook Jesus's desire to come and help us. What would our parenting look like throughout the day if we just stopped and said, *Jesus! I need You to do this specific thing for me. I need You to bring peace because I feel unsettled. Or I need You to show me how to handle this meltdown.* What if we stopped and said to Jesus, *I need You to give me an extra measure of patience, because I am running low.* What if we came to Jesus, petitioning Him with our every need?

I believe that we would find the same willing Savior who says, *You have the ability to ask for My help anytime. I will come. I want you to know that I care about each need from great to small. Don't come to Me only for the big stuff. Throughout your day, turn to Me and say, "Help!" And trust that I will. I don't need you to prove that you can take care of it all on your own. Your request for My help testifies about your faith in Me. When you come to Me asking for My counsel, strength, healing, or help, it proves that you know I can do it. It is My joy to be with you and supply all your needs.*

Lord, thank You for being willing to come and help us. Remind us of Your willingness every time we start to try to do it on our own. Asking for help is not a sign of our weakness, but an acknowledgment of Your strength. We want to prove You are strong and with us. In Jesus's name we pray. Amen.

Yesterday Doesn't Define You, Daughter

Jesus Speaks to the Woman Who Anoints Him

Luke 7

We were driving through our new town when my three-year-old pointed to the car wash and said, "Do you remember when we went there, Mommy?!" I laughed a little, because of course I remembered it. It was just the day before! "I sure do remember, buddy!" I answered him. For my son, the day before seemed like a long time ago.

I wish I could say I was so quick to put events in the past. As a momma, I have a hard time letting go of guilt. Maybe I yelled at my kids or I didn't have enough grace for them. Maybe I chose not to stay with them at bedtime and rushed off to five extra minutes of free time before I collapsed into bed myself. Each moment when I believe that I could have made a better choice or done something differently follows me around, relentlessly playing over and over in my heart. Rather than give myself grace and move on from these moments, I store them up and cycle back through like a playlist of failures highlighting all my not-so-great behaviors.

I'm just not very good at leaving the past in the past. Unlike my son's yesterday, which seemed so far away to him, my yesterday hangs over my head, never quite letting me move on.

If there was ever a woman in Scripture, however, who was able to detach herself from the guilt of her past and move on in her relationship with the Lord, it was a woman spoken of in Luke's gospel. This nameless woman was known by those in her community as a sinner. She had a past that likely wasn't very pretty, yet when she learned where Jesus would be eating, she went to him with an alabaster jar of perfume. As she stood behind him at his feet weeping, she began to wet his feet with her tears. Then she wiped them with her hair, kissed them and poured perfume on them.[77]

The Lord turned to those in the room and acknowledged her sacrifice. But Luke also records that Jesus said to this woman, "Your sins are forgiven. . . . Your faith has saved you; go in peace."[78]

Her great love in this act of worship proved that she recognized what Jesus had to offer. It proved that she understood who God was to her and who she wasn't any longer.

Shame always sets out to remind us of our yesterday. Shame's only job is to tell us that we are the sum of our mistakes. But something powerful happens in the midst of our worship. Our focus on Jesus's love causes us to look at Him instead of ourselves. It shifts our focus from our failure to our Father.

This woman, in the presence of Jesus, did not come away horrified at who she had been. She spent her time glorifying who God was. I believe that is the key to overcoming our guilt. It is found in the face of grace. It's found by looking at our Lord and reminding our hearts that He died so we could be free, and it's important that we live that way.

As we worship, the Lord reminds us, *Your sins are forgiven. Your faith in*

Me continues to save you from the pain of your past. Keep focused right here. Remain at My feet. Yesterday doesn't define you, daughter. Let your love for me remind the Enemy that you know who you are and you know who I am. And then turn back, go in peace, and love your family with freedom.

Let's pause right here together and decide to shift our attention from our failure to the Father's face.

Lord, when guilt would cause us to look at who we were, we stand in the shadow of Your cross and declare that we are free and new creations in You. Help us remember to run to You when the Enemy is chasing us with guilt. And help us remember that we are always received in love and promised the gift of new mercies every morning. In Jesus's name we pray. Amen.

Nothing Is Too Difficult for Me

Jesus Speaks to a Crowded Room

Luke 5

Do you know what I believe? I believe that we only have to see Jesus do something in our lives one time to know that He can do anything. Would you say this is true? Have you ever needed healing in your body, a financial breakthrough, or an answer to come quickly? Have you ever needed the Lord to move in a very specific way and then witnessed as He did? Those moments where we experience God's faithfulness raise the level of what we expect God can do in the future.

When Jared and I were trying to find a place to live in California, we had a certain number of days to secure a rental before we had to be out of our house in Oklahoma. It felt like there was a giant ticking clock that hung over our heads and followed us around. But we had faith that the Lord would do it because we had already experienced His supernatural provision at other times in our lives. He had come through for us before, so we knew that He could and would do it again.

And He did.

If you took a few minutes to think back, I'm sure that you could make a list of the times the Lord showed Himself faithful and able to provide for you and your family. Perhaps it was a timely word from a friend when you had to make a decision or a situation with work or your transportation or your family. Whatever those moments were for you, they created a foundation of faith you can build on in the future.

In Luke 5 we read the story of some people who experienced some foundational faith formation. You've likely heard this story before. Some men were gathered in a house with Jesus, and it was so crowded that there wasn't enough room for a group of men to carry their sick friend to Jesus. These resourceful fellows went up onto the roof, cut a hole, and lowered the sick man down in front of the Lord.

When Jesus saw their faith, He said to the man, "Friend, your sins are forgiven."[79] Wait. Why wouldn't Jesus just heal the man's body? Why did He forgive his sins? The teachers of law and the proud religious law keepers thought the same thing. "Who is this fellow who speaks blasphemy? Who can forgive sins but God alone?"[80]

"Jesus knew what they were thinking and asked, 'Why are you thinking these things in your hearts? Which is easier: to say, "Your sins are forgiven," or to say, "Get up and walk"?'"[81]

But look at what Jesus did. He said, "'I want you to know that the Son of Man has authority on earth to forgive sins.' So he said to the paralyzed man, 'I tell you, get up, take your mat and go home.' Immediately he stood up in front of them, took what he had been lying on and went home praising God."[82]

Do you see what happened here? Jesus can just as easily forgive sins as He can heal bodies, but not everyone understands this. Because you can't see someone's sins forgiven, but you can see someone's body healed, the Lord first forgave the man's sins and then proved that He was capable of doing both by healing the man's body.

What took place in that house was just as much for those who doubted the power and the authority of God as it was for the man who received his physical and spiritual healing. As a matter of fact, Scripture says that before the men lowered their friend to Jesus, while Jesus was teaching, some proud religious law keepers and teachers of the Law were sitting by Him, and "the power of the Lord was present to heal them."[83] Do you see? The power of the Lord was there to heal them. Jesus was showing that nothing is too difficult for Him.

That remains true of our God today. Nothing is too difficult for Him. And to us, I believe He'd say, *I still have all power and authority. I am still fully able to meet your every need. I know you trust Me to forgive your sins. I know you trust that we will spend eternity together, but healing and provision and peace and strength are just as easy for Me to offer you as eternal life. Why do you only believe I will provide part of it? I didn't just come to make a way for you to have eternal life. I came that you might have abundant life right now. Trust Me with all of it. Trust that no area of your life is too difficult for Me to heal and restore.*

Lord, bring to our remembrance every time that You have been faithful to us. And as these moments return to our hearts, allow them to become a foundation for our continued trust that nothing is too difficult for You. We don't just trust You with our souls; we trust You with our lives because Your Son died for all of it. In Jesus's name we pray. Amen.

The Holy Spirit Will Teach You What to Say

Jesus Advises His Disciples

Luke 12

The day my son went to kindergarten, I did my best to hold it together—but I ended up a sobbing mess as I walked him into the school. How did my baby get so grown up? Kindergarten met at the big elementary school. He wasn't even in a separate building. It was just too much. I wanted to just walk nonchalantly through the halls all morning peeking into his classroom every time I passed. But, praise the Lord, the school doesn't allow random adults to just hang out in the hallways, even if their babies are starting kindergarten.

I got the schedule from the teacher, and when I knew they'd be at lunch, I did slowly drive through the parking lot to try to see my kid on the playground. *Is he okay? Does he have friends to play with? Is everyone being kind? Is he drinking water? Would it be okay if I just came and played too?* So many questions.

But do you know what I ended up doing? I ended up praying for my son using the schedule the teacher had given me. I prayed for him when I knew the morning stretch would feel like it was dragging on and lunch would never come. I prayed that he'd find friends at recess. I prayed as the day got closer to the end that he wouldn't miss me too much. It was as if I had a cheat sheet telling me what my son might need and when.

Wouldn't it be great if we had something like that all the time? Wouldn't it be wonderful if no matter where our children were, we could somehow know exactly what to pray for them? Life might not pass out prayer schedules, but we have something even more valuable. We have the wisdom of the Holy Spirit who lives within us and who lives within our children. God literally can be two places at once, taking care of our kids and prompting our hearts to know exactly how to lift them up in prayer.

When Jesus was giving His disciples some advice about what to do when they were questioned by those in religious authority, He said to them, "Do not worry about how you will defend yourselves or what you will say, for the Holy Spirit will teach you at that time what you should say."[84]

This works with prayer as well. We might not know what our kids need when they are away from us. We might not know exactly what they're facing. But the Holy Spirit knows, and Jesus tells us that He will teach us in the moment what we should pray. I know that you worry when your kids are away from you. I know you worry about things like school and friends' houses and even extracurricular activities. I know you worry about what your kids are doing at their grandparents' home or perhaps even with your ex-spouse. But God doesn't leave your children because they have left your sight. God remains with them, caring for them, and teaching us exactly how to cover them in prayer, even from a distance.

One of the hardest things we do as parents is learn to let go little by little. I'm so glad that we serve a God who never lets go of us or our kids. A God who says to us as they leave our arms and remain in His, *I'm not letting them go. I've* got them. *I love them even more than you do, and I know it's hard to allow your children to grow and be brave away from you, but I've given you the gift of strategic prayer. I have sent My Holy Spirit to teach you exactly what to say and when so that your children don't just have Me; they have a momma who can pray in the moment with the wisdom and insight of My spirit. You can trust Me with your kids because I'm the One who trusted them into your care.*

This week, let's be moms who don't wait and worry; let's be moms who armor up and pray.

Lord, thank You for giving us the power of prayer! We often forget that worrying doesn't get us anywhere, but prayer has a powerful impact on everything! Help us listen carefully to the Holy Spirit as He guides and directs us in all things. In Jesus's name we pray. Amen.

The Rhythm of My Heart Is Steady

Jesus Speaks to the Storm

Mark 4

The chair steadily rocked back and forth in the quiet nursery. It was early afternoon, and my youngest was overdue for a nap. His eyelids were getting heavier, but every few minutes he would force them open, just to make sure I was still there.

We moved together back and forth until it became harder and harder for him to force his eyes open, and he finally drifted off to sleep. Truthfully, I had waited all afternoon for naptime. I had a million things I needed to get done, but we were so comfortable together.

So I kept rocking the same steady rhythm even after he was asleep for two reasons: I wanted to soak up a few extra minutes just holding him, and I knew that if I changed the rhythm too abruptly he would likely wake up.

I don't think anyone realizes just how important rhythm is until she becomes a parent. From the steady vibrations of the car that lull a baby to sleep to the soft sway of a new momma's arms or the bouncing shushes when fever or new teeth come unexpectedly in the middle of the night, movement can calm and soothe and ease even the fussiest of dispositions. But the wrong movement? It can be unsettling.

In Mark, we read about the time Jesus's disciples found themselves surrounded by uneasy motion. Jesus had suggested that they all go over to the other side of the lake together. While they were still on their way, a fierce storm came up, and the waves broke over the boat, so that it was nearly swamped.

All the while, Jesus was in the stern, sleeping on a cushion.

Terrified, the disciples woke Him and said to Him, "Teacher, don't you care if we drown?"

Jesus got up, rebuked the wind and said to the waves, "'Quiet! Be still!' Then the wind died down and it was completely calm." Then, Jesus said to His friends, "Why are you so afraid? Do you still have no faith?"[85]

These friends weren't strangers to Jesus. According to Mark, these men had watched Jesus drive out unclean spirits, heal a man with leprosy, heal a paralytic and forgive his sins, and heal a man with a shriveled hand. Firsthand, these men saw miracle after miracle. They knew who was in the boat with them, but when the steady rhythm of the water changed, they became afraid.

Perhaps they didn't yet realize that the same One who hovered over the waters at Creation was riding on the water with them in the boat. Perhaps they didn't understand that the One who set the entire world in motion wasn't going to be moved by a sudden change of rhythm.

But we have the privilege of knowing what the disciples didn't. We know that God Himself holds us in every season and through every storm. We know that He is the One who sets the steady rhythm for our lives, even when everything around us suddenly changes. And just as Jesus declares peace to uneasy waters, we know that He declares peace over uneasy hearts.

Today, I believe He's saying to us, *Why are you so afraid? When rhythms shift, don't you know that I was the One who set this world spinning? Don't you know that nothing moves Me other than your love? You don't have to keep peeking to make sure I'm still here. I am with you. I am holding you. My presence alone is the promise of peace. And when everything else seems out of sync, remember that the rhythm of My heart is steady and endures forever.*

When we find the cadence of our lives in His secure heartbeat, no sudden changes will seem unsettling.

Lord, we can be so much like Your friends in the boat, desperate for You to speak to our storms and calm them. But God, in desperate moments teach us how to hold our peace, knowing that our peace doesn't come from a steady sky or a steady life but from a steady God. In Jesus's name we pray. Amen.

I Know When It Will Happen

Jesus Speaks to the Woman with the Issue of Blood

Luke 8

I was just a day away from my surgery. It would be a fairly quick procedure, but I was admittedly a little nervous. The bleeding had always been intense, but the pain had become excruciating. I was glad to finally have these issues addressed.

I was walking through my living room when I heard in my heart, *Ten thirty-six.*

I wasn't sure what that time meant, but since I was scheduled to go into surgery at 9:45 the next morning, I figured I would be right in the middle of surgery about then. I even told some friends and family, "I need you to be praying at 10:36. There's something about that time, and I think the Lord wanted me to know it would be significant for a certain reason. Just please be in prayer."

The next morning, we arrived at the hospital at the designated time, two hours early as they had recommended. I was prepped and given my IV. But 9:45 came and went. So did 10:00, 10:15, and 10:30.

As it turned out the operating room was busy, and they were running behind, but at exactly 10:36, they walked through the door to take me to surgery.

I couldn't believe it. God had seen this precise moment before it happened, because He knows every moment of our lives.

In Luke 8, we read about a woman who had been bleeding for twelve years. In addition to the illness and physical symptoms of her sickness, at that time bleeding meant that she was considered unclean. No one could touch her and no one could touch anywhere she had been without becoming unclean as well.

She was probably alone most of the time. It's believed that she didn't have any children, and Scripture says that she had used all her resources trying to find a cure. This precious woman was out of options. She was desperate. But Jesus was traveling nearby.

The crowds at this point were crushing Him. He was pressed against and surrounded on all sides, but this woman bravely left her home, fought her way through the people, came up behind Jesus, and touched the edge of His cloak. At that moment, she was instantly healed. Jesus stopped and asked, "Who touched me?" When everyone denied it, Jesus said, "Someone touched me; I know that power has gone out from me."

Then the woman, seeing that she could not go unnoticed, came trembling and fell at his feet. In the presence of all the people, she told why she had touched Him and how she had been instantly healed. Then He said to her, "Daughter, your faith has healed you. Go in peace."[86]

For twelve years this woman had been bleeding. For twelve years she had been weak and desperate. I bet she cried out to the Lord, "When, God?! When will it be my turn? When will you intervene?" But in one moment that Jesus had seen long before she saw Him coming down the dusty road near Jerusalem, this woman was healed. Her appointed time had come.

When Jesus healed this woman publicly, He didn't just stop and acknowledge what had happened for the sake of the crowd there that day. He pointed out this woman's healing for you and me today. He did it so that two thousand years later we could confidently know that Jesus cares about the issues women face. He addressed this issue publicly so that you and I would know that He can heal us too.

I don't know if you're facing infertility or have experienced miscarriage. Perhaps you have endometriosis or heavy bleeding. Maybe every month you're in excruciating physical pain or deep heartache because you're still not pregnant. Maybe you suffer from something that is completely unrelated. I don't know your heart's cry, but the Lord does, and I believe He would say to us, *I see you. I see everything you're facing. I know you need Me, and I know the exact minute on the clock when your healing will come, when your issue will be resolved, when hope will rise. Trust Me. Have faith in Me. I am good.*

Whether it has been a month or twelve years, God sees in advance the exact moment you will encounter His overwhelming love and perfect power. And when the world says things should happen in a certain timing, we will choose to instead trust the Lord's.

Lord, there is nothing more perfect than Your timing in our lives. We trust that You know every second and that You know the precise moment when healing and strength and hope is ours through You. We love You, Lord. In Jesus's name we pray. Amen.

Don't Follow Fear

Jesus Invites Peter onto the Water

Matthew 14

---

*I*t was late at night, and I was terrified about the call to the doctor I needed to make the next morning. I don't know about you, but the most creative moments of my life are the ones when I'm coming up with the list of things that could potentially go wrong. That list gets pretty imaginative. Fear was so loud that night. *What if . . . what if . . . what if . . . ?* I worried.

But fear isn't always as obvious as it was that night. In my life I have noticed that fear can sidle up silently and with a hushed invitation ask me to follow. Often, without hesitation, I do. I follow a trail of toxic thoughts, and before I know it, I'm not just afraid; I am convinced that what I'm afraid of is real.

This is what fear does. Our Enemy shows up and quietly invites us to take one small step after another away from peace until we look around and wonder, *How did I end up way out here?* Have you ever done that? Wondered, *How did I get so afraid of this?*

The truth is, we have a continual invitation to decide who we will follow. Will we follow Jesus when He says, "Follow Me"? Or will we follow fear?

Remember the moment that Jesus invited Peter to step out of the boat and onto the water? Everyone else thought that Jesus was a ghost, but Peter knew his

Lord, and he said, "Lord, if it's you, . . . tell me to come to you on the water."[87]

Jesus answered one word, "Come,"[88] and Peter climbed out of the boat. He recognized the voice. It was the same voice that had invited Peter out of another boat to be a fisher of men. He knew how to follow that voice. But in the midst of it all, in the middle of following the Lord where He had instructed Peter to go, fear showed up again, and Peter began to sink.

However, Scripture says that immediately Jesus reached out his hand and caught him. "Why did you doubt?" Jesus asked Peter.[89]

Today, I feel like the Lord asks us the same thing. *Why do you doubt? Why do you let fear win? Why do you follow fear when you know who I am? When fear invites you to give away your peace, don't do it. Follow Me instead. Follow Me because I love you. Follow Me because you trust Me. Follow Me because I know your tomorrow, and I can safely lead you.*

He's not shaming us. He's offering us a better way. He's reminding us not to become sidetracked on our journey. Like a parent who sees his child approached by a dangerous stranger, the Lord reminds us not to follow someone who desires to lead us away from His love and safety.

Lord, we make the decision right now not just to follow You with our words and actions, but to follow You with our thoughts. Your Word says that we have the mind of Christ. Continue to teach us to think the way You do. In Jesus's name we pray. Amen.

Bring the Kids Too

Jesus Says Let the Little Children Come to Me

John 5; Matthew 19

I sent a quick text message to a friend asking if we could bring our kids to the party. I wasn't sure they were invited since it was an adult's birthday. After a few minutes, she replied that they were welcome to come. I was glad because we didn't have a sitter and we really wanted to go.

As parents, we encounter situations where children keep us from participating with friends or going to events the way we might have before they came along. Early bedtimes and the unavailability of someone to watch our kids means that we might have to turn down invitations and say no more often than we'd like. We constantly have to ask ourselves, "Is this a kid-friendly event?"

But can I say something super honest here? I think a lot of us view the time we spend in prayer or the time we spend reading the Word as "adults only." I don't mean that we tell our children that they have to go away so that we can pray or read. I definitely don't mean that we are getting a sitter just so we can read the Bible.

I just mean that when many of us think of pausing to spend time in God's presence, we look for moments when we are alone. We think of how we can find time without the kids so that we can focus. There is nothing wrong with wanting to be free from distractions so that we can spend time fully tuned into the voice of the Father, but I believe our children need to see us read the Word. They need to see us pray when things get hard. They need to see us stop and ask the Lord for direction and insight right where we are.

Our children need to witness their parents' relationship with God and not just eat the fruit of this relationship. Think of it. Reading the Word and spending time in prayer while our children are in the room is like allowing our children to watch us garden. Children have a deeper appreciation for food when they know how it's grown. When our kids watch us spend time with Jesus, they will begin to understand that our love of God grows when we spend time in His presence.

Jesus knew the value of children watching their parents. As He was teaching, many people questioned His authority. But He told them, "Very truly I tell you, the Son can do nothing by himself; he can do only what he sees his Father doing, because whatever the Father does the Son also does. For the Father loves the Son and shows him all he does."[90]

Everything that Jesus did on earth, He saw the Father do in heaven. Every healing, every teaching, every encounter that Jesus had with people was because the Father had revealed these things to Him. Jesus personally knows the impact of a parent who demonstrates how to be the light of the world.

I think this is one of the reasons that He made a point to say, "Let the little children come to me"[91] as He was teaching. The disciples thought they were protecting Jesus's time with the adults, but Jesus knew that time with Him is not an adults-only party. Children need to be brought into His presence as well.

When we do more than teach our children about God, when we show them what it looks like to worship Him, to be led by Him, and to read His Word, we are doing what our Father in heaven did. We are showing our children how to be more like Him.

He's saying to us the same thing He said to the disciples, *Let the children come to Me. Let them hear the Word. Let them encounter the Word. Let them watch you as you meet with Me. This is not something you have to do in private. This is not something you have to do distraction free. This is a family meeting. As you model for them what it looks like for an adult to be a lover of My presence, you give them something to practice now and replicate when they're grown.*

Finding time to spend with the Lord can be hard in seasons of constant going, but when we bring our children to the party too, we are doing eternal kingdom work. That just might change how we look at studying the Word in the presence of our kids.

Lord, let us be lovers of Your presence in the sight of our children. Let us bring them with us to Your table as we feast on Your Word. Help us see training them to follow You as the more important work rather than a distraction in our time spent with You. In Jesus's name we pray. Amen.

Give Me Five Minutes

Jesus Speaks About the Hungry Crowd

Matthew 15

I nuked those little golden dinosaur-shaped bites for a minute and a half in the microwave and cut up some grapes. I poured glasses of milk. I set the food down in front of the kids, and I fed the baby. This was a typical lunch in the middle of another chaotically messy day with three very small kids.

When they were all done eating, I started the process of cleaning up the kitchen. Since the baby would need to go down for a nap when he finished nursing, cleaning up lunch just meant moving everything closer to the kitchen sink.

In the process, I grabbed the last of the nuggets on their plates and ate the kids' leftovers. One and a half nuggets and about five grapes made up my first and only meal for the day.

I have a feeling that this scene is common in many homes. You might be feeding your kids a different variety of food, but during those years of caring for little ones, so many of us are surviving on leftovers.

We survive on leftover food and leftover time. We gather up what everyone else hasn't consumed yet, and we try to feed ourselves. We don't just do this with food or alone time. Most of us never have time for a full meal of God's Word when every second of each day seems to be accounted for as we care for others.

In theory, waking up before the kids is ideal. But when you have a toddler who ends up in your bed and is sleeping lightly beside you, creeping out to the living room to read the Bible just doesn't always work. Staying up later can feel impossible when you fall asleep in the kids' beds, trying to wait for them to finally close their eyes.

In my kids' early years, this reality created a space for guilt to grow in me. I would think of how long it had been since I opened the Word and really took in what God was saying. I would think of how hungry I felt, and how much I craved that good Bread of Life, but I just didn't know how to make it work. The one thing my heart needed most felt the most impossible to reach.

There's a story in Scripture about a big crowd that had followed Jesus for days. Jesus looked around at them and said to His disciples,

"I have compassion for these people; they have already been with me three days and have nothing to eat. I do not want to send them away hungry, or they may collapse on the way."

His disciples answered, "Where could we get enough bread in this remote place to feed such a crowd?"

"How many loaves do you have?" Jesus asked.

"Seven," they replied, "and a few small fish."

He told the crowd to sit down on the ground. Then he took the seven loaves and the fish, and when he had given thanks, he broke them and gave them to the disciples, and they in turn to the people. They all ate and were satisfied.[92]

God pays attention to hunger, and not just physical hunger. He notices when we are in need of healing, help, and spiritual nourishment. He wants us to have more than enough. But I think we forget that Jesus can take what little we have and multiply it when we place it in His hands.

I believe that just as Jesus can take a few loaves of bread and some fish and turn them into a feast, God can take the few minutes that we offer Him and turn them into enough fuel to keep us going.

I don't believe that Jesus laughs at this offering. No. I think He looks around our lives and gracefully says, *Don't despise what little you can offer. Don't look at it and believe that because it's not more already it won't ever be enough. Don't ignore what you have been given and fail to offer it to Me, thinking it's not going to be what you need so why even bother. Give Me your five minutes, and watch as I multiply the power of the truth you take into your heart.*

In this season, you might not have time for thirty minutes in the Word, but you might have time for three minutes at your kitchen counter while the kids play and watch you or at your desk in between meetings. You might have tiny pockets of time to give to Jesus instead of to Instagram. Read His Word, remembering that He can create a meal out of what you offer Him. Everything is multiplied in the hands of the Lord.

Lord, thank You for the compassion You show toward hunger. In certain seasons we don't have time to dig deeply into Your Word and spend hours digesting Your Truth. Thank You for keeping us fed by multiplying what we can offer You. We thank You for love shown in this way. In Jesus's name. Amen.

I Know Who You Are

Jesus Reveals Peter's New Identity

Matthew 16

I have herbs growing in my kitchen window right now. We are eating mostly organic foods, and we have eliminated all dyes, artificial flavors, and chemicals from our diets. We made this change because we noticed our kids had certain side effects from artificial ingredients, and we believed it would be best to offer them a cleaner diet. But I have to be honest, this new lifestyle isn't one that I used to have or ever planned to have. It's weird being this mom. It's weird being this version of myself.

Because I used to be the mom who handed her kids an entire bag of cheese-flavored chips caked with artificial flavoring and colors and said, "Here's your snack." I might still be that mom if the food hadn't affected my kids the way it did. But here we are. I make 99 percent of our meals from scratch here at our house, and it's still so strange to me.

As moms, we grow in ways we didn't see coming to better our kids and ourselves. We make choices we feel are right in each season as they come, even if we never intended to make them. I think we expect this from our children, but we don't always expect it from ourselves. It's like we know our kids are going to grow, but we forget that we are always growing as well.

I think as moms, we sometimes need to give ourselves permission to grow. We need to remember that it's okay to change—even if that change means we become the mom who is picking her own spices from the planter in the window. Maybe we need to give ourselves permission to change into the mom who goes back to work after years at home or the mom who leaves her job to come home after spending years in school. Whatever the shift, we need to give ourselves permission to change into the person God always knew we would become in this season of our lives.

I like to think about Jesus's disciples and how they were all living other lives before they were called and invited to follow the Lord. We know that Peter was a fisherman by trade. Jesus called Peter to leave a boat and said that He would make Peter a fisher of men. And just like that, Peter's season shifted, and he went from catching fish to following Jesus.

There's a moment recorded in Matthew 16. Jesus was talking with His disciples and asked, "Who do people say the Son of Man is?" and the disciples answered Him. Jesus then asked, "Who do you say that I am?" And Peter, full of the Holy Spirit, identified Jesus by His newly revealed truth. "You are the Messiah, the Son of the living God."

Jesus replied, "Blessed are you, Simon son of Jonah, for this was not revealed to you by flesh and blood, but by my Father in heaven. And I tell you that you are Peter, and on this rock I will build My church, and the gates of Hades will not overcome it. I will give you the keys of the kingdom of heaven; whatever you bind on earth will be bound in heaven, and whatever you loose on earth will be loosed in heaven."[93]

Talk about an identity shift. Peter was stepping into a whole new season, and the kingdom of God needed him to be okay with the change. The kingdom needed Peter to give himself permission to not remain a fisherman forever.

We don't always know what God has in store for us, but we need to give ourselves permission to allow the Lord to change us, to grow us, to invite us on new adventures with Him.

I believe He'd say to us, *I know exactly who you are in every season. You are My daughter, and I have so many good things still in store for you. I need you to stay moldable. I need you to be okay with changing how you think and how you make certain choices. I need you to be okay with transforming for My purposes and My cause. You can trust that because I'm the One doing the shifting, I know what is best for you and for those you love. Yield to the transformation. When you look around and don't recognize who you are in the middle of these circumstances, know that who I am in you will never change. I am the anchor that holds your heart steady in every shifting season.*

Lord, we are clay in Your hands. Whoever You need us to be in this season, we trust You. Whatever changes You need to make, we create a space for You to make them. In Jesus's name we pray. Amen.

Only One Thing Is Needed

Jesus Speaks to Martha

Luke 10

---

*W*ould you imagine with me for just a second? Don't close your eyes, because you need to keep reading, but do your best to picture this. Your kids are being quiet. They're okay. Nothing to worry about. Maybe they're taking a nap or they're at school. Maybe they're playing quietly by some miracle, but you're alone, and the house is mostly quiet.

You're standing at the kitchen sink, and there's a counter full of dirty dishes. The dishwasher is already full, so if these are going to get done, they'll have to be washed by hand. This isn't the only thing that you need to do. Baskets of laundry beckon you from the other room—as do toys and craft projects and a million things that aren't yours but would be easier to take care of yourself rather than wait for someone else to move.

You're trying your hardest not to get overwhelmed. You need to keep going. So you're just focusing on the dishes for now. You're busy sudsing plates and rinsing out cups, and you're making slow but steady process.

But you're not alone. Seated quietly at your kitchen table is Jesus. He's not in a hurry. He's not going anywhere. He's just waiting. When you finish the dishes, He'll move with you into the living room as you sort clothes and fold towels. From there, He'll walk with you as you pick up toys and shoes and move backpacks and check folders. He's never far away. He's just there, but through it all, you don't speak with Him.

Can you imagine it? Can you imagine how ridiculous it would be if Jesus Himself walked into our homes and we just ignored Him all day? You would never, right? Except, we both need to admit that we probably do this more than we care to say. The Lord is always with us, but so often we get so distracted by our work that we forget to talk with Him.

You know the story about the two sisters named Mary and Martha. Luke is the only gospel writer to include their story in his gospel. Luke records that Jesus was traveling, and Martha opened her home to Him. Mary sat at Jesus's feet, "but Martha was distracted by all the preparations that had to be made. She came to him and asked, 'Lord, don't you care that my sister has left me to do the work by myself? Tell her to help me!'

"'Martha, Martha,' the Lord answered, 'you are worried and upset about many things, but few things are needed—or indeed only one. Mary has chosen what is better, and it will not be taken away from her.'"[94]

If you're like me, you've often thought, *I'd never get so distracted by my work that I would miss Jesus. I'd never think dishes were more important than time spent in the presence of my King.* But here we are, you and I, modern-day Marthas choosing all the work before the worship.

So often when we read this story, we see it as though there are two options. We can either work, or we can spend time with Jesus. As if it's one or the other. But the truth is, we have unlimited access to the Spirit of God. We don't have to choose. We can have conversations with Jesus at the kitchen sink. We can worship Him and love on Him and let His presence push back fear and discouragement while we fold the towels. We can do everything we need to do while spending time at His feet.

Today, I believe the Lord would gently remind our hearts, *One thing is needed. Only one. Because if you have Me, then you have everything you need to take care of everything else. Let Me be a part of your day today. Let Me give you strength. Remember, I never leave you.*

Where is He in the room with you right now? Can you see Him?

Lord, we're so sorry for all the times we let our busyness distract us from the most important work of our lives. Retrain our hearts to sense and remember Your presence in even the most mundane aspects of our day. Thank You for never leaving us. In Jesus's name we pray. Amen.

I'm Awake in the Middle of the Night Too

Jesus Speaks to Nicodemus

John 3

When my little ones were newborns, I spent most of my nights awake. I firmly believe there is a supernatural strength that God gives women when they become mothers, because there is no other way a human could operate on so little sleep and so much stress. While my husband did his best to help, many nights I would be the only one awake. Well, other than the baby.

Those newborn days weren't the only time I would find myself awake at night. As my babies grew, I would wake up with restless toddlers or a sick little boy or a potty-training little girl. Stress, worry, fear, my schedule, my responsibilities . . . all stole some of my rest as well. But no matter what kept me awake, I noticed one thing about the middle of the night. Night can be so dark and lonely.

My children have grown, and I now lie awake struggling with different issues. I wrestle with hard questions, and I wonder how God is going to fulfill certain promises. Night—the time we are supposed to finally be resting—can be the most restless.

In Scripture, we see that Nicodemus, who was a member of the Jewish ruling council, came to Jesus at night. He asked Jesus many hard questions. He said, "We know that you are a teacher who has come from God. For no one could perform the signs you are doing if God were not with him."[95] But Nicodemus continued to probe the Lord, asking, "How does this work?" "What exactly do you mean, Jesus?" "What are you saying?" And Jesus responded to Nicodemus, answering each question as it came.

This moment in the middle of the night is when Jesus famously said, "For God so loved the world that he gave his one and only Son, that whoever believes in him shall not perish but have eternal life. For God did not send his Son into the world to condemn the world, but to save the world through him. Whoever believes in him is not condemned, but whoever does not believe stands condemned already because they have not believed in the name of God's one and only Son."[96]

These words weren't proclaimed from a mountainside. They weren't spoken only to Jesus's best friends. They weren't declared as Jesus made His way to the cross. This foundational truth of our salvation was spoken at night by the Lord to a man struggling with his faith.

We likely bring different questions before the Lord, but see, Jesus didn't reject Nicodemus in the middle of the night. He didn't say, "You know what? You need rest, and I need rest. This isn't the time. Come back later. Let's talk about this tomorrow." No. Nicodemus was awake and so was Jesus. Jesus met Nicodemus right where he was, answering the hard stuff, explaining the mysteries of the world, and being present in the moment with this man full of questions.

Jesus took time for Nicodemus in the middle of the night, and He takes time to address our deep concerns in the middle of the night as well. While He speaks to our individual needs, I believe the Lord also says to all of us, *I know it* feels lonely when the world is quiet and there's no one to talk to. I know that in moments like these, your thoughts can be so loud. But I don't shy away from your running mind. I don't reject your questioning. I chase after you, calming your fears, explaining what I can, and bringing you peace so that you can rest knowing that I am God and I am with you and you are so very loved.

Praise the Lord that we have a God who doesn't sleep.

Lord, You called out to Samuel in the night, and You met with Nicodemus at night. Your presence is the same no matter the hour. When we are kept up for any reason, remind our hearts that we are in good company. In Jesus's name we pray. Amen.

You Need a Good Drink

Jesus Speaks to the Samaritan Woman

John 4

I think the last time I was bored was in 2005. No kids. No husband. No mortgage. I was mostly just concerned with keeping my summer tan and making sure my MySpace account stayed up to date. Those were easy days.

Today I am needed from the time I wake up until well after everyone is asleep. Long after my children are tucked into bed, this pile of laundry looks over at me from the couch. "Hey, girl, I need someone to take care of me too." My family needs me. My work needs me. My house needs me. I do my best to keep up with everyone and everything, but I always feel like I'm chasing *finished.* I wonder if it's possible that my work will ever actually be done because it feels like the finish line is continually being moved just out of my reach. It's like a marathon that I didn't prep for but that I'm required to run. I'm tired a lot.

And if I'm being honest, I feel like most of the time I'm "Just a second"-ing everyone and everything I love. "Just a second, Mommy's helping sissy right now." "Just a second, Mommy's getting dinner into the oven." "Just a second, microwave, stop beeping at me!" "Just a second, husband, I'll be there when I'm done with this." And worst of all, *Just a second, Jesus, I want to give You my full attention, so let me do everything else and then we can sit and talk.*

One of my favorite stories in Scripture is of the Samaritan woman who came to draw water from the well in the middle of the day. We can speculate plenty about her life just by looking at the time of day she went to get the water, since most women would have gone in the morning in the cool of the day. Perhaps she went in the afternoon to avoid the other women. Perhaps she just couldn't take their whispering or ugliness; she had previously had five husbands and the other women all knew it. Or perhaps she was just running behind that morning. Who knows?

All we know for certain is that when she arrived, Jesus said to her, "Will you give me a drink?"[97] This was a big deal because the Samaritans didn't talk to the Jews, and it was even more audacious for a Jewish man to speak to a Samaritan woman. The woman pointed this out, and Jesus answered, "If you knew the gift of God and who it is that asks you for a drink, you would have asked him and he would have given you living water."[98]

This is what Jesus offers us as well. We know that Jesus is never far away, but I often picture the Lord as like the people who run alongside marathon runners, handing them water and shouting, "Keep going!"

This is the type of access we have to the fountain that never runs dry. We might always be a little bit tired. No matter how much exercise we get or how many vitamins we take or how healthy we try to stay, there is a constant drain in the areas where life is poured from us. But we don't have to remain empty. We have access to One who offers living water who would say to us today, *You need a drink of My living water. I'll stay close. You drink deeply. Don't try everything on your own. The One whom you are speaking to is the Savior you need, not just in eternity, but in your day-to-day. I have come to rescue you from the exhaustion of doing it on your own. Let me be the strength your family seeks through you.*

156

Lord, in response to Your loving-kindness that never runs out, our hearts say, "Yes, we will remember our Source." We will remember to stop throughout the day and drink deeply from Your love so that we can be what our families need. Thank You for never running dry. In Jesus's name we pray. Amen.

Trust Me at My Word

Jesus Speaks to the Royal Official

John 4

Have you ever heard someone say, "God said it. I believe it. That settles it." This last year has confirmed that I need more people in my life with that kind of belief. Because I have discovered that I'm personally more of a "God said it. I believe it. But I'm going to question it a few times before I decide if I'm all in or part of the way in" kind of girl. Do you know what I mean?

Don't get me wrong. I want to have a settled heart. I want to take Jesus at His word, but most of the time I would prefer to take Jesus at His sign, His miracle, or His visible presence in my life.

Last year, God invited Jared and me on the incredible adventure of moving our family to California. That makes it sound so romantic and exciting. Really, it was faith testing and terrifying most of the time. Yet we moved our three kids across the country because we believed we heard God say to do it.

From my perspective now, I can see exactly how He arranged this to work in His timing and perfect plans. But on the other side of it? Back when we didn't know how He intended to provide for us, I was very unsure. There were plenty of nights I stayed awake questioning if His word was actually strong enough to hold all of us. I remember crying, *Can I really trust You with this move, God?!*

Maybe you've never been asked to move across the country, or maybe you have. Maybe your moments of faith-testing tribulation were the result of a health crisis or job transfer. Maybe God asked you to go back to work or to leave a one-in-a-lifetime dream job to be with your kids. Perhaps God asked you to start your own business or go back to school. There was a moment for each of us when God prompted our hearts, and we decided if we would trust Him at His word alone.

There's a story in Scripture about an unnamed father with a sick son. We don't get many details about this family. We only know this man was a royal official with a gravely ill boy. Knowing that Jesus could heal his son, this father went to find Jesus and bring Him back with him.

He said to the Lord, "Sir, come down before my child dies."

"Go," Jesus replied. "Your son will live."

And in that exact moment, this father had to decide if Jesus's word was enough.

Scripture says, "The man took Jesus at his word and departed. While he was still on the way, his servants met him with the news that his boy was living. When he inquired as to the time when his son got better, they said to him, 'Yesterday, at one in the afternoon, the fever left him.'

"Then the father realized that this was the exact time at which Jesus had said to him, 'Your son will live.' So he and his whole household believed."[99]

When I think of this story, I'm not sure I could do what the father did. Could I walk away without Jesus, carrying only His word instead?

The truth is, the Lord has already spoken promises over each of our lives. He has spoken the promise of peace and the promise of His hope and the promise of His presence. He has spoken the promise of His faithfulness to us. In both big and small moments, the Lord speaks life over our hearts. But do we act as though it is as good as done?

Today, I feel like the Lord would ask us the same question. *Will you take Me at My word? Will you live as though I made a way for you to have life and have it abundantly? Your spirit will live and not die. You've been raised to life in Me, and that means you don't ever have to be afraid. I am the Word, and you can trust Me.*

Friend, I don't know what specific assignments and dreams the Lord has spoken over your life, but I know that His word is good. Today, let's decide to settle that once and for all.

Lord, You have never given us a reason not to trust You. Whether through a big adventure or the simple acts of daily obedience, help us remember that if You said it, it is as good as done. In Jesus's name we pray. Amen.

What Do You Really Want?

Jesus Speaks to Blind Bartimaeus

Mark 10

For the last few weeks, I have been chasing a clean house. I told myself that if my house was clean, I'd have more peace and my family would be happier. Clean was the goal. Except my son got the flu, and then the other two kids got the flu, and then my husband and I both got the flu, and everything that I had worked so hard to create seemed to disintegrate overnight.

When we overcame the sickness, I had to start all the way over, stripping beds and washing sheets, disinfecting everything, doing the dishes and washing the clothes, and putting everything back together again. It was bigger than one day. It was day after day of chasing the goal of trying to put everything in its place.

Late one night, exhausted after doing my best and still falling short, I prayed, *Lord, if You could just help me catch up, then everything would be better. I just need help catching up.* And I felt the Lord asking me in return, *Is that what it would take for you to have peace in your heart? You need your house put in order first? What is it you really want from Me?*

I thought about what I was really asking. I wasn't asking for peace, I was asking God to create circumstances around me that I believed would create the peace. I think sometimes we have to consider what we really want from the Lord when He asks us, *What do you want Me to do for you?* These are the exact words that Jesus said to a blind man named Bartimaeus.

Scripture says that Bartimaeus sat near the side of the road between two towns. When Jesus passed by, this man shouted out,

"Son of David, have pity on me!"

Jesus stopped and said, "Call him over!"

They called out to the blind man and said, "Don't be afraid! Come on! He is calling for you." The man threw off his coat as he jumped up and ran to Jesus.

Jesus asked, "What do you want me to do for you?"[100]

(I love this. I love that Jesus asked the blind man what he wanted. Isn't it obvious, Jesus? The man wants a tropical drink and vacation. No, the blind man obviously wants to see. Yet, Jesus asked him.)

The blind man answered, "Master, I want to see!"[101]

Jesus told him, "You may go. Your eyes are healed because of your faith."

Right away the man could see, and he went down the road with Jesus.[102]

Something very important and telling happens right here at the end of this story. The blind man wasn't just satisfied with having sight. He used his sight to follow Jesus.

You know, sometimes we think if we had exactly what we always wanted we would finally be happy. But there's such a profound lesson in this blind man's request. When he got what he always wanted, he didn't stay where he had always been. He used his new sight to follow Jesus, because Jesus is what really satisfies our hearts. Jesus is what our hearts really crave.

Do you know what the Enemy wants you to believe? He wants you to believe that if you finally had *that thing* you'd be happy. If you were finally healthy, if your marriage was secure, if you made *x* amount of money or had that debt cancelled. If you finally had what you wanted, your heart would be whole.

But it's all a lie. It's the lure to distract you from pursuing what will truly satisfy. Those things we'd like to have might be good and worthy of attention, but they don't fill our hearts the way Jesus can. And at the end of the day, a redecorated house or a refilled closet or a rejuvenated mind or body isn't the ticket to peace. Jesus is. And when we properly place Him on that aching throne of our hearts, we realize that it was His presence that was missing all along.

Yet Jesus asks us, *Do you really think you need your house to be clean to have peace? Do you really feel you need a certain amount of money in the bank? Do you really believe that you need anything other than Me?* Waiting to give us what we really want, Jesus asks, *What is it that I can do for you?*

The reply we should be prepared to answer always is *Lord, I want to be able to follow You. Don't allow anything to keep me from Your presence.*

Because it's His strength and His provision and His peace and His love that fulfill the longing in our hearts.

Lord, when we become distracted by what we need, help us refocus on what You have made available to us. We want more than just our vision. We want to be able to see that following You is best. Position our hearts to seek You in all things, knowing that from You flows everything else we need. In Jesus's name we pray. Amen.

Let's Go Talk Alone

Jesus Speaks to Zacchaeus

Luke 19

We were at a friend's birthday party one evening when one of my children got upset about something silly. This child had been winding up for a breakdown all day. Has your child ever done that? Where you can almost feel the meltdown coming, and you're just waiting to see where it finally happens and under what circumstances? I was just glad that we had made it to the party, but about halfway through it, there were tears, there was very little reasoning, and it felt like all our friends were watching this entire situation unfold.

So I took this precious child of mine outside, and we sat on the steps of the house we were visiting. We waited for the heat of the moment to pass and for this child to become reasonable again. When everything cooled, and when my child's little heart calmed and we were able to talk through what happened not only at the party but also at home leading up to the party, we were able to resolve the issue and return to our friends.

Sometimes situations with my children need to be addressed in the moment, wherever they are taking place. But other times my children need a quiet retreat to process their feelings away from the watchful eyes of those who might not understand. As a parent, I do my best to keep my children from having to experience shame as they work through their heart issues. I do my best to take my children someplace alone so they don't have to wear the weight of other's opinions of their behavior.

Our God is kind that way too. After Jesus healed Bartimaeus, He continued into the town of Jericho. We know that Bartimaeus decided to follow Jesus after he received his sight, but he wasn't the only person walking along with our Lord. Scripture says there was a huge crowd that followed Jesus as He traveled. The crowd was so big that a man named Zacchaeus had to climb a tree just to see Jesus.

"When Jesus reached the spot, he looked up and said to him, 'Zacchaeus, come down immediately. I must stay at your house today.' So he came down at once and welcomed him gladly."[103]

We don't know what happened at Zacchaeus's house. We aren't told if anyone else was there with them, even though we could assume the disciples stayed with the Lord. All we know is that after a private conversation, Zacchaeus, who was a tax collector, "stood up and said to the Lord, 'Look, Lord! Here and now I give half of my possessions to the poor, and if I have cheated anybody out of anything, I will pay back four times the amount.'

"Jesus said to him, 'Today salvation has come to this house, because this man, too, is a son of Abraham. For the Son of Man came to seek and to save the lost.'"[104]

Jesus did not use Zacchaeus to teach the crowd of people a lesson. He didn't say, "Everyone! Look at this guy in the tree! He's a sinner! Don't be like this guy!" No, the only thing Jesus did publicly was accept this man and say, "Come down! I must stay at your house today." Alone and away from the crowd, the transformation took place in Zacchaeus's heart.

I'm so thankful that the Lord does this with us as well. He doesn't use our faults or failures to make a public mockery of us. He invites us into private dialogue where we can address the things that are keeping us from living the life that God intended for us. Alone with our Lord, we can deal with the heart issues that Jesus already knows about.

If you're dealing with shame, if you've got some things that need to be worked on, I think you'll hear the Lord inviting you to come away with Him for some one-on-one time. I think you'll find that the Lord is saying, *Come on! Let's go talk about this someplace quiet. Let's go sit together until your heart feels better. Let's work on this before we go back to the party.* And in that place of quiet refuge, we can find healing and freedom from everything that has been troubling us. Praise the Lord that we serve a God who doesn't shame us into submission but compassionately cultivates a relationship to lead us into healing.

Lord, we know we have things that we need to work on. Thank You for loving us in such a way that we can deal with those areas in our lives in a private way alone with You. You're such a good Dad and we love You so much. In Jesus's name we pray. Amen.

I Don't Condemn You

Jesus Speaks to the Woman Caught in Adultery

John 8
---

*H*e brings me before the Lord and throws me to the ground. "Look at this woman! She yelled at her kids! She lost her patience. She's full of bitterness and unforgiveness. She's a continual disappointment to You, Lord. She's a terrible mother and wife and friend. What would you say should be done to her? What is her punishment?" I wait for the verdict, hearing clearly the voice of my accuser, but straining my heart to make out the voice of the Lord. I look up and lock eyes with my Savior. There's so much grace that meets me in that space. Grace that I don't deserve. Grace that flows like healing honey. Grace that sets me on my feet so I can try again.

There's a story in Scripture of a woman who was caught in adultery. Those who found her brought her to Jesus while He was teaching. Her accusers said that the law of Moses demanded that she be stoned. Trying to trap Jesus with condemnation, they said,

"In the Law Moses commanded us to stone such women. Now what do you say?" . . .

But Jesus bent down and started to write on the ground with his finger. When they kept on questioning him, he straightened up and said to them, "Let any one of you who is without sin be the first to throw a stone at her."[105]

One by one they left until it was just Jesus and this woman remaining.

Jesus straightened up and asked her, "Woman, where are they? Has no one condemned you?"

"No one, sir," she said.

"Then neither do I condemn you," Jesus declared. "Go now and leave your life of sin.'"[106]

Often, we come before Jesus ashamed. We come with feelings of guilt. We come ready to be reminded of our unworthiness by the Enemy who wants us to fail.

But Jesus looks at us and He remembers that He already took care of our accuser on the cross. Today He's not bending down to write in the sand until everyone leaves us alone, as He did in His encounter with the woman caught in adultery. When we accepted Him as our Savior, He wrote with His blood the verdict that says, "Not guilty."

He's standing eye to eye with us now, looking at us as daughters and not as disappointments. He made the payment for each one of our failures when we entered into a relationship with Him. This grace isn't permission to fail Him continually and avoid doing as He says, but this grace is permission to live in the freedom that He already paid for without the tormenting accusations that we are unworthy.

Friend, He took care of our accuser, so why do we still condemn ourselves? Why do we live full of shame and regret and deep guilt? Why do we allow our Enemy to bring us shamefully before the One who paid the price for each of our failures?

I believe just as Jesus spoke to that woman, He is saying to each of us, *Where are your accusers? Daughter, neither do I condemn you. Get up. Get going. Sin no more. And make the decision to stop remaining here on the ground, defeated by your shame. Choose to live in the freedom I paid for on the cross. Choose to stop living in guilt and live in the grace I made available to you. Your family needs you to get up out of your shame. Your family needs you to accept this forgiveness so that you can move forward. Because guilt doesn't just impact your heart. It keeps you from becoming the woman I created you to be. And this steals from your family. Don't let your shame take from those you love too.*

When we accepted Jesus as our Savior, His blood declared, "Not guilty." Maybe it's time we stop arguing with him.

Lord, help us see ourselves as You do. Help us love our families enough to release ourselves from the guilt that seeks to bind us. Help us fight for our families by fighting the guilt that wants to cripple and steal our joy. Your joy is our strength. Help us replace the thoughts of guilt with acceptance of grace. In Jesus's name we pray. Amen.

You Don't Know What You're Asking Me

Jesus Speaks to the Disciples' Mom

Matthew 20

I don't know about you, but whenever I take my kids to Chick-fil-A, they eat half of their food in the restaurant and the other half of their food on the road "to go." It could have something to do with the play place, but I'll take a few nugget crumbs in the car if it means I can have five minutes to eat my lunch in peace while they play. I've seen other moms leaving the restaurant with their uneaten nugget boxes stacked tall like a brick wall, so I know I'm not the only one whose kids eat the last few bites on the ride home.

This usually works out just fine, except one afternoon when Kadence was very young. We went to eat at Chick-fil-A before we ran a few errands in the neighboring town, and when Kadence didn't quite finish her meal, I took her food with us as usual. I expected she'd eat it on our way to our first stop. When we arrived at the store, we got out, took care of what we needed to, and then got in the car to head home. Kadence saw her nugget box and asked for her leftovers, but I couldn't say yes. It had been hours since we first ordered our meal, and the nuggets had been left in the car. By my estimation, it had been far too long for her to eat it safely. The food that was good just a few hours before had spoiled, and I had to tell her no.

"But I just really want it!" she demanded.

"But you don't understand, baby. It's just not good for you," I consoled her.

I could totally relate. There have been moments in my life where I have screamed at God.

"Please!!! Why won't you give it to me?! I want it!!!"

The truth is, sometimes we want what seems good to us, but we don't really know what we're asking the Lord to give us. Thankfully, God is merciful and doesn't give us everything we perceive to be good. This is what the mother of two of Jesus's disciples learned the day she knelt before the Lord and asked for a favor.

" 'What is it you want?' he asked.

"She said, 'Grant that one of these two sons of mine may sit at your right and the other at your left in your kingdom.'

" 'You don't know what you are asking,' Jesus said to them. 'Can you drink the cup I am going to drink?' "[107]

Jesus knew what was coming for Him. Jesus knew that He would die on a gory cross and in doing so, would drink from the cup of God's wrath poured out on Him for all sin.

This mom didn't realize just what she was asking Jesus. Jesus seems to make it clear that in order for her sons to have this favored place in His Kingdom, they'd have to go through what He was about to endure.

From her perspective, she was asking for something good and honorable for her sons, but Jesus knew the cost of those positions in heaven.

I think that sometimes we ask the Lord for things that we perceive to be good and then wonder why He won't grant our simple requests. Like my daughter, we ask, "Why won't You just give it to me, God? It seems good to me!" And we are often too upset to hear Him gently replying, *You don't get it. You're asking Me to give you something that would cause you harm. You're asking Me to say yes when this would bring you pain. So I can't grant your request because I love you too much to give you something that would harm you. I love you too much to give you what isn't best.*

I don't know what you've asked the Lord for specifically now or in the past, but I do know that His answers are always for our good.

Lord, in our lives, our perspective is not always the same as Yours. We don't always see what You see or know what You know. Give us grace to say okay when you tell us no. Help us remember that You're always protecting, always loving, and always upholding us because You're a good God. In Jesus's name we pray. Amen.

It Was Because I Love You

Jesus Speaks to the Disciples About Lazarus

John 11

One rainy morning not so long ago, my husband took Kolton to school. Knowing Kolton would have to spend a few minutes on the playground before he went inside, my husband decided to leave the umbrella with him. Unfortunately for me (who would be in charge of pickup), it was still raining when the day was over, and we only owned one umbrella.

As my other two kids and I climbed out of the car and began the walk up the hill to pick up Kolton, I thought about how great it would be if it stopped raining for just a few minutes. Kadence had the same idea.

"Mommy, I prayed, but Jesus didn't make it stop raining."

With rain pouring off the end of my nose and my shirt soaked through my jacket, I recognized this as a teachable moment.

"Sometimes someone else needs the rain more than we need it to be dry," I answered her.

After spending the last seven years in a farming community, we didn't dare pray for the rain to stop. We knew how much life depended on that rain.

I was thinking of the story in which Jesus raises Lazarus from the dead.

While Lazarus was still sick, his sisters sent word to Jesus. Scripture says,

"When he heard this, Jesus said, 'This sickness will not end in death. No, it is for God's glory so that God's Son may be glorified through it.' Now Jesus loved Martha and her sister and Lazarus. So when he heard that Lazarus was sick, he stayed where he was two more days."[108]

Wait. Jesus loved them, and so He stayed before He came to them? This isn't quite what I imagine when I think of love. To me it would make more sense for Scripture to say, "Jesus loved them, so He ran to them and healed Lazarus."

But that's not how this story goes. After two days, Jesus told His disciples, " 'Our friend Lazarus has fallen asleep; but I am going there to wake him up.' . . . Jesus had been speaking of his death, but his disciples thought he meant natural sleep. So then he told them plainly, 'Lazarus is dead, and for your sake I am glad I was not there, so that you may believe. But let us go to him.' "[109]

For your sake, I'm glad I wasn't there . . . so that you may believe.

You know, I can imagine the intense prayers said by Mary and Martha and their close friends. I can imagine the desperation they felt for their brother. But Jesus didn't answer the way they wanted. He didn't come running. And Lazarus died.

But that's because this was never supposed to be a story of healing. This was always supposed to be a story of resurrection. God didn't come when Mary and Martha asked because he wasn't just going to bring Lazarus back to life. He was going to bring the hearts of those who witnessed this miracle back to life as well. But no one understood this until Lazarus walked out of the tomb.

I suppose in our lives, there are moments when we say, *Why aren't You acting right now, Lord? Why aren't You answering the way I want You to? Why are You delaying Your response, God? Why is it still raining?*

And in those moments, I believe the Lord is saying to each of us what He said to the disciples, *It is for your sake and for My glory that I am not answering the way you hoped. It is because I am good that I am not just healing but resurrecting. Life will come from this. And just as I loved Mary and Martha and Lazarus, I love you and that's why I am waiting.*

Because we are in the middle of the story, we don't always have the opportunity to understand the why. But friend, we can still understand the heart of the Father and trust Him in the middle of it. We can look back on the story of Lazarus and remember that the same God loves us the same way.

Why is it still raining when I prayed, Momma? I suppose the best answer is because He loves us.

Lord, we don't always understand Your purposes, but today we choose to remember that You are always motived by love. It is because You love us that you answer us as You do. Help us see the opportunity for resurrection of dreams, hope, and life in every situation. In Jesus's name we pray. Amen.

Take Away the Stone

Jesus Speaks to Those at Lazarus's Tomb

John 11

For the last two years, we have had a pet hamster named Hammy. That hamster lived through some pretty interesting circumstances. He survived a trip out and about the night that I accidentally left his cage open before my son started first grade. He survived escaping from his cage and finding his way onto a sticky trap while we briefly stayed with my in-laws before we moved. And Hammy survived a two-day trip across the country.

So when we noticed a small growth on Hammy's tummy, we weren't too worried. We thought that whatever it was would be one more obstacle that Hammy easily overcame. Except the growth just got bigger and Hammy began to struggle to do basic things like climb through his tubes and crawl into his food dish.

I found a vet and scheduled an appointment. Unfortunately, our fears were confirmed. Hammy had a fast-growing tumor, and when the abscess on his stomach grew too large, he would suffer and pass away. We didn't want the little guy to go through something like that, so we decided to have him put to sleep.

As they took him away, I started to cry. I felt silly. It was just a hamster. It wasn't a friend or a loved one. But the vet leaned over and said, "It's really okay to feel sad." And something about the permission she gave me to experience the moment just as it was allowed me to cry harder.

You know, I think sometimes we feel like our sadness needs to be justified and rushed. As if sadness doesn't deserve to be felt and needs to end quickly so we can get back to being happy and experiencing joy. But sadness has a purpose of its own. It reveals the compassion we feel for others. It reveals the love we felt for what's gone. It causes us to reach out to hope, and ultimately sadness often compels us to take action to fix what's hurting. When Lazarus died, Jesus displayed the importance of pausing to weep.

When Jesus came near the home of Lazarus, Mary, Lazarus's sister, "fell at his feet and said, 'Lord, if you had been here, my brother would not have died.'

"When Jesus saw her weeping, and the Jews who had come along with her also weeping, he was deeply moved in spirit and troubled. 'Where have you laid him?' he asked.

"'Come and see, Lord,' they replied."[110]

The Bible then records the shortest verse in all of Scripture. "Jesus wept."[111]

It's so important that we read those words in relationship to this story, because it shows us that even Jesus paused to express sorrow. Even Jesus, the Resurrection and the Life, the one who would bring Lazarus back from the dead, stopped to weep at the brokenness of this world before moving forward. Weeping isn't a sign of weakness. Sadness isn't a sign of sin. Jesus's tears revealed the deep love and compassion He felt for His friend.

But His tears also teach us something else important. They teach us that we have a sympathetic Savior. Scripture goes on to say that, "Jesus, once more deeply moved, came to the tomb. . . . 'Take away the stone,' he said."[112]

And Lazarus came back to the land of the living.

In the middle of everything else, Jesus didn't say, "Why are you all crying? Don't you have faith enough to know who I am?" He didn't rush people through their emotions. He felt sadness alongside everyone else. There are words that Jesus says in Scripture that we need to hear through the filter of His compassion. We need to listen for the tone of God's heart. Imagine the tears still in His eyes. Perhaps His voice cracked a little. With a wet face and real beating heart, the Savior of the world called out to Lazarus, and he came back to life.

I hear the Lord reminding us, *I understand the pain of being human and experiencing death. I don't love as someone far off. I love as someone who knows and who comes close. When you grieve, when your heart hurts, when you're sad, know that I have wept with you.*

It's important that we experience a triumphant Savior declaring Truth over our circumstances, but we need to also remember that we have a God a who understands exactly how we feel even when we grieve.

Lord, thank You for not leaving us in our sorrow but coming and sitting alongside us. Teach us how to use the sadness we experience to propel us into deeper relationship with You and others. Allow moments of sorrow to be opportunities to extend Your love. In Jesus's name we pray. Amen.

You Play a Part in This Too

Jesus Speaks to Lazarus

John 11

*H*ow do I muster the motivation to take care of any of it?" It was one of those kinds of mornings. My younger two kids had woken up at 5:00 a.m. after going to bed late the night before. Everyone was crabby, myself included. My house was a disaster, I had a million things to do, and I just didn't know where the energy would come from to deal with any of it.

I threw out a simple prayer: *Lord, You're going to have to get me out of this funk. I just don't know how to shake it today.*

I walked into the kitchen and started to cook myself a nice breakfast—something I rarely do. I might grab a bite with the kids, but I don't scramble eggs and make sausage patties and pop bread into the toaster every morning. (Hands up for the cereal club!) I played some worship music as I cooked. I sang out loud. I invited the Holy Spirit to fill my heart and my home. And I reset my morning by feeding my body and my spirit. Jesus did the reviving, but I had to make the choice to contribute. I had to walk out the miracle of a transformed day. I had a part to play.

I think that sometimes we forget that we are involved in our own freedom. We are involved in our own healing. We are involved in our own miracles. What do I mean? Jesus transforms our hearts daily. Jesus does the resurrecting and redeeming in our lives, and it's up to us to walk it out. If we want a better day, we have to make certain choices and move forward to create one. If we want to stop feeling angry with our spouse, we have to make the choice to extend grace and forgiveness before he earns it. If we want to feel less critical of the world around us, we have to decide to have compassion and love instead.

Ultimately, we all want to be free from what would keep us bound. We want to be free from frustration and lack of motivation and resentment. And the Lord wants to perform these miracles in our lives. He is calling us out of every trap the Enemy has laid to steal from our lives, but we have to put our faith in Him in action.

The moment that Jesus shouted to Lazarus from outside his tomb, Lazarus came back to life. Lazarus was awake and breathing, but he was still wrapped and bound in a dark tomb. Jesus said, "Lazarus, come out,"[113] and in that moment, it was up to Lazarus to walk out what Jesus had begun. Jesus did the resurrecting; Lazarus did the walking.

I know that I can get caught in that dark tomb, waiting for someone to come in and get me, while the Enemy tells me it's too much work to get up and move forward. But really, Jesus is calling to all of us. *Get out of your funk. Get out of your discouragement. Get out of your moodiness and your crabbiness and everything else that would steal your life from you. Don't you hear Me calling to you? Don't you know that I'm the Resurrection and the Life? Abundant life is already yours. Freedom is yours. Hope for today is yours. I've already made a way for you. Now, it's up to you to decide if you're going to take steps toward what I have already provided.*

We might begin our day saying, *God, I don't know how you're going to get me out of this,* but I believe the Lord kindly reminds us to trust Him and take the first step.

Lord, thank You for calling us out of the places where our hearts get stuck. God, we can forget that You paid a high price for us to be free to live with joy and hope and promise. Lord, I want to see You get what You paid for when it comes to my life. You paid for complete freedom. Help me wake up and walk out of every place where the Enemy would keep me tied up mentally, spiritually, and emotionally. Give me the strength to take each step forward. In Jesus's name I pray. Amen.

I Understand What You've Sacrificed

Jesus Speaks About Mary

Matthew 26

---

*I*n the beginning, the sacrifice is expected. As mothers, we sacrifice our sleep so that our children are fed and changed and safe. We sacrifice our rest and our time and the attention we could give to ourselves to instead care for our sweet babies. Others notice this sacrifice. They ask us about our sacrifice. They encourage us to recognize the value in what we are doing. But as our children grow, the sacrifice isn't always as understood.

"Why would you go back to work when you have a baby at home who needs you?" someone might ask the mother who is going to work to provide for that baby at home. "Why would you give up that incredible opportunity to stay at home with your baby?" someone might ask the woman who would sacrifice her career for more time at home with her little love. And where often the sacrifices we make to care for our children are misunderstood, sometimes they are even missed altogether.

Rarely does anyone see the missed sleep to care for the six-year-old battling anxiety at night. Rarely does anyone see the missed meals as we race from our meeting to take our kids to their practice. Rarely does anyone see the missed personal friendships as we spend our days taking care of little ones with special needs. Rarely does anyone recognize the continual sacrifice that comes along with motherhood.

But I think of the moment that a woman named Mary took her entire life savings in the form of a jar of perfume and poured it on Jesus's head. And I think how others questioned this kind of reckless love and reckless giving and the Lord stopped them and said, "Why are you bothering this woman? She has done a beautiful thing to me. The poor you will always have with you, but you will not always have me. When she poured this perfume on my body, she did it to prepare me for burial."[114]

He was explaining something profound in these two sentences. He was explaining that Mary's offering was a part of God's plan for Jesus's final days, but He was also saying to everyone in the room, "While you fail to see what she's really sacrificing here, I see the value and I understand just what this cost."

That is what I believe He wants us to know today as well. I believe that God sees the sacrifice of your life. He sees the way you give it all for the ones you love and do it as an act of worship to the Lord.

When no one else recognizes all you do, when you're up in the middle of the night or going without for the sake of your kids, when you're pouring out your life for those around you, I believe the Lord says to you, *I recognize the value of what you've given. I see the importance of your offering. I know what deep sacrifices you have made for the ones you love, and I honor them. I understand the measure of what you've poured out for the sake of love.*

Because if anyone knows about a life poured out for others, it is Jesus. And if His love has taught us anything, it is that the sacrifice is always worth the gain.

Lord, thank You for being the One who sees our hearts. When no one else appreciates or seems to value what we do, God, You say that what we do is significant. You know the love shown through sacrifice. Your sacrifice made it possible for us to know You. Thank You for sending Your Son. Thank You for helping us see the worth in what we do. May every act of love point back to Your love, and may every moment we sacrifice for others remind us of the Great Love that sacrificed for us. In Jesus's name we pray. Amen.

Let Me Wash Away the Dust of the Day

Jesus Says He Must Wash the Disciples' Feet

John 13

I scooped him up and put him into the bath and knelt beside the tub as he splashed and kicked. I loved to give Jaxton baths. I loved to give all my children baths. Really, it was always my favorite time of day with my littles. Even though by the end of the day I was absolutely exhausted, once I got the kids into the tub, I always loved lathering up a little rag and washing away the dust of the day. We'd laugh and sing and blow bubbles off our hands. Some nights were less fun and more work. Some nights as I knelt on the floor of the bathroom, I got just as wet as they did. But looking back now, when those nights of washing babies are over, those really were some precious times. I was just a momma getting her babies clean. But I didn't see how much I was acting like Jesus in those moments.

So much happened on the night Jesus was betrayed and began the final steps to the cross. Scripture says that Jesus and His twelve disciples had gathered in a room and that Jesus got up from the meal they were sharing, "took off his outer clothing, and wrapped a towel around his waist. After that he poured water into a basin and began to wash his disciples' feet, drying them with the towel that was wrapped around him."[115]

When He came to Peter, Peter questioned Jesus and then said, "No, . . . you shall never wash my feet."[116] Peter must have felt a sense of unworthiness. Perhaps Peter thought, "Who am I, that You should stoop to wash the dirt from me?"

However, Jesus answered Peter, "Unless I wash you, you have no part with me."[117] Jesus wasn't just telling Peter about dusty toes here. Jesus was revealing a far more important Truth. Unless He cleanses us from our sins, we will have no fellowship with Him. In that moment as water met dirt, Jesus was speaking of His blood washing away what had separated us from His love.

We can be so much like Peter though, can't we? Hesitant to allow God anywhere near our mess, we think, "Who am I that I should bother You, God, with all this dirt? I'm completely unworthy to even be in Your presence."

Yet the purpose of Jesus going to the cross was to wash us and restore us into right relationship with His Father. When we listen to the voice of the Enemy saying we don't deserve to be in the presence of God because we are such a mess, we are denying the truth that God died just so He could cleanse us and bring us back to Him.

Without the dust, there's no reason for the washing. We can be confident that God's not afraid of the messy areas of our lives. He already took care of them on the cross. His purposes are declared every time we allow the water of His Word to rinse our soiled spirits. And I believe that it's His delight. It's the precious promise of a Savior who would stoop to wash feet to remind us that He would come down from heaven to cleanse hearts. God delights when water meets mess.

Today, let's listen as the Father speaks these words over our hearts. I believe

He's saying, *Daughter, it is My joy when the water of My Word washes away the dust of your day. Unless I cleanse you, you won't have freedom. So don't hold back from Me. Don't refuse to allow Me to do what I came to do. I am the King who came just to bend down and do what no one else could. I came to wash you and make you whole.*

I love thinking back on giving my babies baths, but when I think of it as picture of God's love washing away the dirt of my life, it makes those moments and those memories so much sweeter.

Lord, when we look at You, we see how unworthy we are. This can make us want to shrink back. Help us remember that it is worship when we come boldly before You and allow You to make us clean. We love You. In Jesus's name we pray. Amen.

Strengthen Your Sisters

Jesus Predicts Peter's Denial

Luke 22

*H*as anyone ever told you, "You're going to miss this?" I'm guessing you've heard that at least once in your life, maybe even once today. Personally, I think that was the hardest thing to hear when I had very young children. I felt like I was in the middle of an endless ocean with no shoreline in sight, just trying not to sink and wondering how I was supposed to keep going. I wanted a life raft. I didn't want someone to shout from the safety of the next season, "Hang on! It will be over before you know it and then you'll be sad it's gone!"

I always thought, "Yeah, sure." *Glug. Glug. Tread. Tread.* "I'll try to enjoy it, because someday I'm going to miss this! Thanks for the advice!"

You and I both know that those words always come from a place of love. Those words always come through the filter of someone who fully understands what it means to miss what they will never have again. But those words do not always encourage.

Can I tell you what would have encouraged me in those years with little ones when the days blurred together and there was no relief in sight? A veteran momma who fully remembered what it felt like to be in that season and offered to help me would have been encouraging. One who remembered not only the snuggles and the sweet stuff but also the picky eaters and fit throwers and sleep stealers that live in this season. I would have given anything for a mom who had been where I was to look back and say, "I see you. Let me come back and offer my strength."

Jesus told Peter to do exactly this with the other disciples. Just before Jesus was about to be taken and crucified, He warned Peter of what he would face.

Jesus said,

> "Satan has asked to sift all of you as wheat. But I have prayed for you, Simon [Peter], that your faith may not fail. And when you have turned back, strengthen your brothers."
>
> But [Peter] replied, "Lord, I am ready to go with you to prison and to death."
>
> Jesus answered, "I tell you, Peter, before the rooster crows today, you will deny three times that you know me."[118]

Often, when we read this story, we focus on Peter's denial, but many of us skip right over Jesus's prayer. Because when Jesus prays for you, it's as good as done. And when Jesus said, "I have prayed that your faith may not fail," Jesus knew that Peter's faith wouldn't fail when he had to live with the consequences of denying the Lord.

It isn't just a story of Peter denying Christ, even though we often make it the focus. In this short conversation, we see that Jesus knew exactly what Peter was about to go through and how it could be used to help his friends later. Through this story we see that Jesus prayed for Peter's faith to be strong, not just for his sake, but also for the sake of the rest of the disciples who would follow him.

I would say that Jesus knows the same is true for each trial we face. You are going through things right now and the Enemy might want your faith to fail, but I believe that Jesus is strengthening you. He's declaring that your faith in Him in this season won't fail. We might question. We might doubt. We might not easily say, "YES! You can get me through this, Jesus!" and in doing so deny in our hearts His ability to be God in our lives. But our faith won't fail. Our lips might question, but our hearts will remain secure.

And I believe that the Lord would say to each of us, *When you get to the other side of this, strengthen your sisters. Use what you have learned to help them, to go back for them, to pull them from the endless ocean of hopelessness. The Enemy has requested to break you, but I have prayed that you'd be strengthened, and when I pray, it's as good as done.*

I know this season feels heavy. But that's because it's not just for you. You're going through this for all the women you will be able to turn and help because of your experience. It feels heavy because you don't even realize how many women you're carrying through this season with you right now.

Lord, strengthen our hearts when we feel hopeless. Send help from those who have already walked this road. And show us where we can go back for others who are currently in seasons that we have passed through. We desire to take what we've learned in previous seasons and use it to help others. In Jesus's name we pray. Amen.

I'm Not Going Anywhere

Jesus Speaks About the Holy Spirit

John 14

When my daughter was younger, she didn't like to go into new situations alone, and she definitely didn't want to remain in them alone. One Sunday morning, I took her to a new Sunday school class at church, promising to stay with her on her first visit. Even though I gave my word that I would not leave without her, she just couldn't convince herself that I wasn't trying to sneak out of the room.

I wanted her to have peace. I didn't want her constantly looking over her shoulder or needing to feel my hand on her back while she colored. I wanted her to relax and enjoy time with her friends.

And then I looked down at my feet and began slipping off my shoes. "Kadence, I'm going to leave my shoes right here next to you. I can't leave the room without my shoes. I will sit over there by the wall, and you can keep my shoes near you while you play and learn. That way you can be sure I'm not trying to leave."

Within minutes, she was playing with the other children, unafraid that I would slip out and leave her behind.

As I sat in that room on a tiny plastic church chair, I thought of how God promised to send the Holy Spirit to His disciples. Jesus knew that He was going away, so before He was crucified He gathered His friends together and promised to send another Comforter. Jesus said, "If you love Me, keep My commandments. And I will pray the Father, and He will give you another Helper, that He may abide with you forever—the Spirit of truth, whom the world cannot receive, because it neither sees Him nor knows Him; but you know Him, for He dwells with you and will be in you. I will not leave you orphans; I will come to you."[119]

It's important to point out that the Greek words used here for "another advocate" are *allos paraklētos*. *Paraklētos* is translated as "helper." The word used for another, *allos,* means "another of the same kind." Look, I know you weren't planning on a Greek lesson today, but track with me for just a second because this is good stuff. When Jesus speaks to His friends here, He tells them that He is sending another Helper of the same kind, one who is just like Him. Jesus is promising that even though it feels like He's leaving, He's not.

Acts 2:39 says that the promise of the Holy Spirit is for "all whom the Lord our God will call." And He calls us. He came for us. Jesus couldn't stay with us, but He sent us His Spirit, who feels and talks and acts just like Jesus, to be with us! When we pray, *Jesus, come close. Jesus, help! Jesus, be near.* It is His Holy Spirit that He sends.

Today He wants to remind our hearts again, *I'm not trying to get away from you. I don't want you to have to figure it out on your own. I want you to know that I have made a way that we can always be together. When you fear that I've left, remember I promised not to leave you alone. When you're afraid you're going to face a situation without Me, remember that My promises cannot be broken. I'm a good Father, and I want to be with you.*

God is in the room where you hold this book, and the room where it was written, and everywhere else there is a child of God. His shoes are off, friend. We don't have to be afraid.

Lord, thank You for staying with us always. There is no future of ours where You are not present. Help us find rest in that. In Jesus's name we pray. Amen.

Nothing Can Keep My Love Away

Jesus Promises to Return

John 14

For weeks we had been preparing for Kadence to go to the dance with her daddy. We had gone shopping for the perfect little dress. We had her hair cut, and we painted her nails. We even ordered a precious little wrist corsage with white flowers that matched the details on her little shiny leather shoes. She had never been to a dance before, and it was all she talked about as the date got closer.

"What kind of music will they play?" "Do you know if my friends are going too?" "Will Daddy really dance with me?"

We had a big calendar with the date circled, and each morning she counted how many days were left.

You might be able to image how devastated she was when she found out that her daddy had to work out of state the weekend of the dance. We honestly weren't sure if Jared's work schedule would allow him to make it or not. We didn't want to commit to one answer or the other, but we explained that her daddy would do his very best to come home in time to take her.

The morning of the dance, we still didn't know if Jared would make it home in time. They had a certain amount of work to accomplish before he was able to leave, and he had a six-hour drive back to our house.

Truthfully, he had every reason not to come considering how exhausted he would be from work and how far he had to drive both ways, but those things don't weigh nearly as much as a daddy's love for his little girl.

That sweet man of mine drove home, got dressed, got the corsage out of the refrigerator, and then went out of the house and rang the doorbell so that he could properly pick up his littlest lady for their very first dance. No other situation or circumstance or obligation outweighed the promise that he made when he said that he would do his best to come for her.

And our Jesus? Well, He feels the same way about us. He shows up just because He loves us, and nothing has the power to keep His love away.

We know that just before He would be taken away from His friends, He told them that He was sending another Comforter, but He went on to say, "I will not leave you as orphans; I will come to you."[120] When we look at this from the perspective of the disciples, we know they had no idea what Jesus would have to endure to come back for them. They had no idea that when Jesus said, "I will come to you," He meant He would defy death, hell, and the grave to get back to them. They had no idea what He would have to go through in order to reach them again. And yet Jesus said He would.

Listen, when a death-defying Jesus says that He will come for us, *He comes for us.* There's nothing that can stop Him. There's nothing that can hold Him back. No power of hell, no circumstance on the earth can stop the Father's love for His children.

The Lord is reminding you and me of His promise today. He's telling us, *I will not leave you as an orphan. I will not leave you fatherless. I will come to you. There's nothing that can hold My love back. There's nothing that can prevent Me from reaching you. Neither death nor life, neither angels nor demons, neither your fears for today nor your worries about tomorrow—not even the powers of hell—can separate you from My love. No power in the sky above or in the earth below—indeed, nothing in all creation will ever be able to separate you from My love. I promised I would come back for you, and I meant it. I am a good God who cannot lie.*

When I think of my husband's face as he scooped up our little girl and carried her out the front door, I know it is just a glimpse of the Father's love for us—a Father who would send His Son to die in order to carry us in His arms again.

Lord, when we feel discouraged, when we feel unlovable, when we just need the reminder, You speak gently to our hearts and tell us that there is nothing that can keep Your love away. Thank You for coming for us when You didn't have to. Teach us how to show this same kind of love to others. In Jesus's name we pray. Amen.

My Peace I Give to You

Jesus Strengthens His Disciples

John 14

I have been afraid for most of my life. I wish that wasn't true. I wish that wasn't part of my story, but as I have come to learn more about the anxiety that often plagues my heart, I realize that it's important for Christian women to bring it from the shadows. Anxiety stems from a number of sources, but the anxiety I face is actually the result of a genetic mutation that affects how my body functions. This genetic mutation is something I was born with, and now that I'm into my thirties, it's something I'm still learning how to manage.

Couldn't Jesus heal me? How can I profess to love and trust Him if I feel afraid so much of the time? Well, Jesus can heal me just as He can heal a paralytic. Make no mistake—I know He is still in the miracle-making business. But I would never ask a paralytic to walk in order to prove his faith in Jesus, and I would never tell a woman who suffers from anxiety to simply stop feeling afraid in order to prove that she believes in the miracle-working power of Jesus. I have great faith, and yet my heart often feels afraid.

This is how I know that my feelings can be liars. My feelings are often at war with what I know to be true. My feelings want me to believe that I should be afraid, when I know in my heart that the Lord is my protection. My feelings want me to believe that it's not going to be okay, when I know in my heart that the Lord is working all things together for the good of those who are called according to His purposes. My feelings want to tell me to hide or avoid, when I know the Lord has asked me to reach out and share. My feelings are real. They point to what I'm experiencing, but they don't always line up with Truth.

Peter experienced something similar. Just before going to the cross, Jesus gave His disciples a gift. Jesus told His friends, "Peace I leave with you; my peace I give you. I do not give to you as the world gives. Do not let your hearts be troubled and do not be afraid."[121]

How could anyone be afraid after Jesus spoke these words directly to him? How could anyone have a troubled heart if Jesus Himself said to them, "I'm leaving you My peace"?

Yet, just hours later, out of fear for his life, Peter denied even knowing Jesus. Peter's feelings caused him to act in a way that was contrary to what his heart knew to be true.

And if this could happen to Peter just moments after Jesus said, "Do not be afraid," what would make us think that we are exempt from feeling afraid or anxious ourselves? What happened to Peter is proof that Jesus can give us good gifts and we can choose not to use them. Peter had access to the peace Jesus offered, but he trusted his emotions more than he held to the Truth.

The same goes for us. Our lack of peace often means that we are choosing to believe our emotions rather than believe the Truth.

So, what do we do? When we are feeling anxious, when we're feeling afraid, when our feelings seem to have a voice of their own, we remember the gift. We listen as the Lord kindly reminds us, *Peace I leave with you; my peace I give you. I do not give to you as the world gives. Do not let your hearts be troubled and do not be afraid.* We hear the voice of Truth telling us, *Listen to Me. Focus on what is True. Focus on My love and My presence. When everything would try to steal what I give freely, remember the gift of My peace. Remember that it's yours to use whenever you need it.*

This is the starting place for our freedom—the gift of peace that is always available to us.

Lord, we do not have any reason to fear, and yet our hearts can become anxious. Bring healing today. Bring hope today. Teach us how to use the give of peace we have been given. In Jesus's name we pray. Amen.

There's a Reason I Didn't Tell You

Jesus Says the Holy Spirit Will Explain

John 16

Can I be honest? If I had known all that would transpire in my family during the course of the last year, I might have purposefully tried to change the trajectory of our lives. If I had known the type of heartache and stress and heavily sad days that would be a part of this move across the country, I might not as easily have said yes when God invited us on this journey. There were hard moments that only God saw coming, yet in His infinite wisdom, He knew that what we gained in the process would be worth our sacrifice.

So He gently guided our hearts right through the middle of often turbulent waters because He knew that we would arrive safely on the other side. Truly, there are things that God knows would be too much for our hearts to bear if He told us on the easy side of it. He knows that there are things that the Holy Spirit will have to guide us through before we know the full story.

When Jesus was telling His disciples goodbye, He said to them in John 16, "I have much more to say to you, more than you can now bear. But when he, the Spirit of truth, comes, he will guide you into all the truth. He will not speak on his own; he will speak only what he hears, and he will tell you what is yet to come."[122]

The truth is, Jesus was fully aware of everything they were about to witness. He knew that they would watch as He was wrongly accused, tortured, and unjustly crucified. He knew that they would watch Him hang on a gory cross with a crown of two-inch thorns pressed into His brow. He knew that He would be mocked, ridiculed, and eventually impaled and placed in a borrowed tomb.

Jesus knew that His followers needed to be prepared for what was coming, but He knew that they couldn't handle the weight of the details. He also knew what was coming for each of them eventually. He knew that many of them would die horrible deaths as well.

But He knew that when they saw Him come back from the dead, when they witnessed not only His death, but His resurrection, they would be able to face anything.

There are some things that Jesus doesn't tell us because He knows they are too much for us, but He doesn't leave us without counsel during this time. He sends His Holy Spirit to guide us and tell us what is yet to come.

This is still one of the jobs of the Holy Spirit in our lives today. He reveals the Truth to us in ways that we can handle, strengthens us for the journey ahead, and equips us to face what is still coming.

I know that sometimes we want answers, and we want answers now. We want to know exactly how it all plays out. We want to know not just what to do next but how to prepare for the years ahead. And sometimes we wonder why, if God is good and if He really loves us, He won't tell us. But sometimes the proof of His love is in His withholding of details.

Sometimes Jesus says to us, *It's too much for you to bear, daughter. It's too much for you to know right now. Because I do know what is coming, I'm asking you to trust Me right here. I'm asking you to trust Me with what I have told you* already. I'm asking you to wait for the Holy Spirit to reveal what's next in a way that you can process and so you can move forward safely. Just because I'm not telling you doesn't mean that I don't know. I know enough—and I know you enough to know that it would be too much.

In these moments, the best response of our hearts isn't to beg for details but to praise the Lord for His merciful silence that leads us steadily on.

Lord, too often we forget that You don't withhold information to tease us. You don't delight in playing games with our hearts. God, You reveal to us what we need to know based on Your good mercy. Help us trust You with this Truth. In Jesus's name we pray. Amen.

I Will Remember My Love for You

Jesus Speaks to the Thief on the Cross

Luke 23

I heard him crying, but it didn't sound quite right. As moms, we quickly learn the difference between "I'm not getting what I want," "I'm angry," and "I'm hurt" and all the other unique-sounding cries of our children. It was the middle of the night, and I was disoriented. We had just moved into our new house. Part of me wanted to take off running toward what is now our bathroom door, but what would have been our hallway door at our previous house. With my eyes still mostly closed, I stumbled down the hall and made my way to his bedroom.

Everything was blurry. Where was he? Why was he crying? Why did he sound so confused? A pile of blankets was on the floor next to his bed, and his bed appeared empty. I got closer and lifted the blankets to find my three-year-old curled up on the floor, still mostly asleep.

His cries were confused because when he had rolled out of bed, he had woken himself up just enough to know that he wasn't where he was supposed to be but not enough to know how he had gotten where he was.

I picked him up, then held him while sitting on the edge of his bed before tucking him back in for the night. It's kind of funny, but it was as if he didn't realize he had fallen until he saw me come to pick him up.

When Jesus was taken to the cross, one of the last conversations He had was with a criminal hanging on a cross next to him. Like the crowd, the man hanging on a cross on one side of Jesus mocked him, but the other criminal rebuked this man.

"Don't you fear God," he said, "since you are under the same sentence? We are punished justly, for we are getting what our deeds deserve. But this man has done nothing wrong."

Then he said, "Jesus, remember me when you come into your kingdom."

Jesus answered him, "Truly I tell you, today you will be with me in paradise."[123]

Jesus was hanging on that cross, willingly taking the punishment of sin upon himself so that neither of those men would have to live eternally separated from God. Yet only one man woke up and realized how far he had fallen.

Only one man said, "Remember me."

But notice how Jesus did not respond to this man who asked to be remembered. Jesus did not say, "Sure, I'll remember you. I will remember every time that you hated your brother, stole from the unsuspecting, and abused the innocent." No. Jesus said, "Today you will be with me in paradise."

I wonder if that man knew that he was in need of rescuing before he found himself hanging next to his Savior. I wonder if he hadn't realized how far he had fallen until Jesus came to scoop him up and save him.

While we are equally guilty and deserving of the consequence of sin, we get to be with our Lord before we pass on into eternity. And when we cry out to Him, when we have fallen and we need His saving grace, when we shout, "Remember me, Jesus! I need Your help!" He doesn't come and point out all our failures in our falling. He doesn't chastise and say, "How'd you get down here anyway?" He doesn't say, "Sure, I'll remember you. I'll remember every time you yelled. I'll remember every time you walked away or scolded your child when he just needed a hug. I'll remember every time you didn't handle it the way that I would."

No. With the same kind of compassion that Jesus offers every child of God, He simply lifts our weary hearts and says, *Sure. I'll remember My love for you that made a way for Me to come. I don't withhold My help, because I remember the cost that was paid so that I'd be able to be here with you. I delight in mercy. I throw your failures into the sea. And I remember your sins no more.*

And He picks us up and puts us back where we belong, sometimes before we even realize how far we've fallen.

Lord, thank You for remembering Your love for us. Sometimes we don't even know how we got to the place where we needed Your help so badly. Help us boldly declare that we need You to remember us, trusting that You will come and set things right. In Jesus's name we pray. Amen.

Your Grief Blinded You

Jesus Speaks to Mary at the Tomb

John 20

*W*hen I woke up with extreme discomfort and some other alarming symptoms just a few weeks after I found out I was pregnant, something inside me knew what was coming. And yet I prayed. I prayed so hard that my fears would not be realized. I prayed so hard for that sweet little life that I already loved so fiercely.

As the baby slipped from my body, it was as if all hope slipped from my body as well. I was hurt, and I was angry. This wasn't how this was supposed to end. And yet as much as I wanted to be angry with God, I refused to blame Him. I needed Him more than ever to comfort my devastated heart. I just wanted to know, "Where were You when all of this was happening?"

Have you ever asked God a similar question? *Where were You exactly, God, when I was going through that?*

I decided to find out where He was when I was going through my moments of loss and heartache. As I prayed and walked back through the previous weeks in my heart, I saw the Lord with me. I saw Him share in my joy when we found out we were pregnant. I saw Him hold me close when the pain began. I saw Him weep and hold us both when the sweet little life was lost.

In the midst of it all, I didn't see Him, but He was there. I had just been blinded by my fear and grief. I am not the first woman to miss Jesus right in front of me because I was so focused on my pain.

John tells the story of the morning Mary Magdalene went to Jesus's tomb and found it empty. Two angels were there and asked why she was crying. She said, "Because they have taken away my Lord, and I don't know where He is." Overcome by grief, she turned to leave and saw someone standing there. It was Jesus, but she didn't recognize him. "Woman, why are you crying?" Jesus asked her. "Who are you looking for?"

She thought He was the gardener. "Sir," she said, "if you have taken him away, tell me where you have put him, and I will go and get him."

"Mary!" Jesus said.

She turned to him and cried out, "Teacher!"[124]

Mary was so overwhelmed by deep sorrow that she didn't even recognize the man she was looking for when He spoke to her.

Grief does this. It blinds us. Grief often requires us to focus on what we have lost, causing us to lose sight of everything and everyone else. Have you ever experienced anything like this?

The truth is, He never left either of us. He didn't leave me during my miscarriage, and He hasn't left you. But . . . we can miss Him. We can miss the realization of His presence surrounding us because of the sorrow or pain that overwhelms us. But, sister, I believe the Lord is calling to us both.

I believe that He is saying, *Why are you questioning My presence when I'm standing right in front of you? Who are you looking for? Because I'm right here. I didn't abandon you, and if you look, I'll tell you exactly where I was every step of the way. You were never alone.*

It can be painful to walk back through previous seasons and ask the Lord to show you where He was, but it can also bring peace and closure. I don't know what you've been through, but I know this: the goodness of God is not changed by the brokenness of this world, and the Lord Himself weeps over your pain and loss.

Lord, forgive us for accusing You of abandoning us when You were right there and we didn't see You. Forgive us for the moments our grief blinded us and we cried out to You, not knowing that You were softly calling to our hearts. Show us where You were when it was scary, God. Show us where You were when it was too much. Show us where You were when we felt all alone. Because we know You were there. Thank You for Your presence. In Jesus's name we pray. Amen.

I Have Proof That You're a Good Mom

Jesus Addresses Thomas's Doubt

John 20

You know, just about every job on the planet requires you to complete a performance review. Your strengths and weaknesses are discussed. The areas where you can improve are addressed, and you walk away with a pretty good understanding of how you're doing.

But nobody does this for us mothers. Other than the judgmental looks of the other moms in the store or the rare moment when someone tells us, "It looks like you're doing a great a job," no one is reviewing us. Some days that's a relief, and other days that's terrifying.

We basically have no idea how we're doing. There's no end-of-the-year summary. There's no benchmark or online scoring system moms can use to calculate how they rate. There's just women doing their best and hoping they're doing enough. This creates an opportunity for the Enemy to sneak in and say, "But you're not enough. You're doing a terrible job. And you should doubt everything you do."

We often listen to him. If we are all being honest, I think most of the time we doubt that we are doing enough. We doubt our abilities. And we doubt that we are actually decent moms.

God has a lot to say about doubt, but one of the most tender moments when God speaks to a sincere questioning heart is found in John 20. The disciples were all gathered together, except for Thomas. Jesus chose this moment to appear to the group of men, and when the disciples later told Thomas that Jesus had been with them, Thomas famously said, "Unless I see in His hands the imprint of the nails, and put my finger into the place of the nails, and put my hand into His side, I will not believe."[125]

Scripture goes on to say that a week later, the disciples were all gathered together again, and this time Thomas was with them. Jesus came to them again and said, " 'Peace be with you.' Then He said to Thomas, 'Reach here with your finger, and see My hands; and reach here your hand and put it into My side; and do not be unbelieving, but believing.' "[126]

Jesus could have said to Thomas, "You know what? You didn't believe your friends. You doubted, and that's just too bad." But He didn't. Jesus extended peace, and then offered proof, saying, "Reach here with you finger. . . . Do not be unbelieving, but believing." Jesus was willing to give Thomas the reassurance he needed. Jesus was willing to offer Thomas the opportunity to enter into full belief.

As moms, we might not have a measuring stick or a chart or any other practical way to gauge our success and believe that we are good moms. But just as Jesus graciously offered Thomas the proof his heart needed, the Lord wants to help our unbelief as well. He wants us to know that the proof of our success is found in His completed work, not ours.

We will fail. We will fall short. But when Jesus died, He made a way for every shortcoming in our lives to be made whole in Him. When He died, He made a way for us to love our families well as we extend His love to them. He made a way for relationships with those we love to be healthy by first restoring our relationship with the Father.

The Enemy would say that we should doubt who we are as moms, that we should doubt how well we are doing, but Jesus graciously says to us, *I have proof that you're a good mom. While the world would measure your success one way, I say that the proof of your success is found in the holes in My hands. When you allow Me to be the center of your home, when you allow My love to be the love that you pour out on your family, when you invite Me to be a part of raising your children, you are allowing Me to be enough for them. You don't have to doubt yourself. You just have to trust that My grace is made perfect in your weakness. When you doubt, remember that I am holding out My hands to help your unbelief.*

Lord, we want to be believers and not doubters. We want to stand as confident moms, ready to measure ourselves by Your standard of grace and not by the Enemy's judgment and condemnation. Thank You for continuing to extend Your hands as the proof of Your love. When we feel like failures, may we point to Your completed work and say, "As long as I'm sharing His love, I'm doing enough." In Jesus's name we pray. Amen.

I Know Who You Are Now

Jesus Invites Peter to Keep Following Him

John 21

Before I was a mom, I was the admissions director at a private Christian university. I worked with students. I had a great team. I got to interact with people, and I really enjoyed my roles in that season.

When I became a mom, so much of my identity changed. I joke that I might hear someone actually call me by my name once a week. Most of the time, I'm Mom, Mommy, or Momma. Who I am now is so different from who I was just a few years ago.

You know, most of the disciples had very different lives before they were invited on an adventure of faith and following Jesus. They were Jewish men who knew about the coming Messiah, but many were fishermen by trade, and Luke was even a doctor.

Life for the disciples must have been so different in those years of transition from who they had previously been to who the Lord was shaping them to be. Yet the Lord was mentoring these men, teaching them how to do what He did, and allowing them to see Him and know Him personally. Jesus was helping the disciples become the men they would be for the rest of their lives.

I imagine the disciples felt very lost after Jesus died. I can only speculate, but after following Jesus daily for years, they must have wondered once He was gone, *What now?*

One night, still unsure of what to do now that he wasn't with Jesus daily anymore, Peter decided to go fishing.

I like to picture the disciples sitting around wondering what to do and Peter standing up and saying, "You know what? I'm going fishing." So he did. Peter and a few of his friends went back to what they knew best.

And that's exactly where the resurrected Jesus showed up again and gave Peter instructions on what to do next. After a breakfast on the shore of fish and bread, Jesus told Peter again, "Follow me."[127] It was the same invitation Peter received when his journey with Jesus began.

I have a feeling that there are days when you don't recognize who you are anymore. You spend so much time taking care of everyone and everything else that you have little to no time to spend alone. You look around and think, "Who is this person who is so unlike who she used to be? I said I would never _____. I thought I would always _____. I didn't see this coming!"

Yet Jesus looks at us and knows us so well. Jesus knows that, like Peter, we can't go back to who we were before, as much as we might like to just be fishermen again. We can only move forward with Him.

So where do we go from here? Like Peter, we wonder, "Who am I now?" I think if we listen closely, we'll hear the Lord saying to us, *Follow Me. You'll become the woman and mother I want to shape you into through time in My presence. You'll become more like Me. Don't you see? You might not be who you were, but who you are was always meant to be discovered in who I am. You're a parent now too. You're beginning to understand My heart and My love from a new perspective. And as you follow Me, you'll keep discovering what it means to be My daughter now that you understand the heart of a Father.*

I know you don't always recognize her when you look in the mirror, but she isn't lost. She is being discovered and becoming more like Jesus through this refining season of motherhood. So long as we keep following Him, we'll know who we are in light of who He is. Daughters of Grace. Carriers of Truth. Lovers of Mercy. Women who have been called to mother children into His kingdom.

Lord, help us learn what it means to be a daughter of God as we now understand more deeply the love of a parent. When the Enemy taunts and says we're lost, give us words to remind him that we are securely found in the person of Jesus Christ. In Jesus's name we pray. Amen.

You Can Try Again

Jesus Restores Peter

John 21

---

*D*o you want to try again?"

I was bent low in the kitchen, eye to eye with my little girl as tears streamed down her face. She was so upset, and she was determined to let me know just how disappointed she felt. The truth is she needed to change her attitude. She needed to reset her heart. She really needed to apologize for her behavior. But more than anything, she needed permission to start over.

I think of this moment with my daughter as I help all three of my children through their fits and frustrations. I think of it in the middle of my own overwhelmed moments. I think of it when I've done something for which I should apologize . . . but would rather pout and feel upset instead. And I think of it anytime I need to be reminded that it's okay to try again.

As moms, we need to experience moments like my daughter's often, and I don't mean only when we have children who need permission to start over. We also need to remember that we don't have to wait for a new day to begin again. We don't have to wait for the sun to rise to have a clean slate or to reset our hearts.

After Peter's betrayal, Jesus offered him the same fresh start. Jesus died and was resurrected on the third day. He appeared to His disciples a number of times, but one of these times was from the shore after the disciples had gone out fishing. He called to them and asked if they had caught anything. When they realized it was Jesus, Peter jumped into the water and swam to Jesus, unable to wait the few extra minutes it would take for the boat to reach Him.

When I read this story, I like to think that I'd be like Peter, jumping into the water like a crazy person and swimming to the beach as fast as I could. But if we think about Peter's last interaction with the Lord while He was still alive, it's amazing to see that Peter did not get stuck in guilt.

He could have been a prisoner to the shame of what he said and did in the hours when his Savior was giving His life for him. He could have stayed back and thought, *I denied Him. Why would He accept me?* But Peter chose the opposite.

He didn't hide. He didn't sulk. He ran . . . okay . . . swam to Jesus. Peter got to Jesus as quickly as he could because Peter knew for certain what we need to remind ourselves of daily. Peter knew that Jesus is the type of friend who reaches out and says, "Let's try again."

Jesus proved this when He offered Peter a moment of reconciliation. Peter had denied Jesus three times, and three times on the shore Jesus asked Peter, "Do you love me?"[128] For each time Peter denied knowing Jesus, Jesus gave Peter a chance to say he did.

Here's the thing. As moms, we need to hear Jesus telling us that we can start over too. In moments when we know we've dropped the ball, lost our temper, or taken something out on our families that didn't even have to do with them, we should take cues from Peter. We should dive headfirst into the ocean of God's grace and get to the side of our Savior as fast as we can. Where guilt says, "It's totally unforgivable. You should just stop even trying to be better. You're always going to be this much of a letdown to those you love most," I imagine the face of my Father as He bends low and looks me in the eye. I imagine His gentle voice saying, *Do you want to try again? I love it when you give yourself permission to start over. I love it when you live in the freedom that I bought on the cross. Don't get stuck in your guilt. Don't sulk in your shame. Come to Me as quickly as you can, knowing that I am ready to receive you and make everything right.*

Our kids need moms who hear God say, *Do you want to try again?* and who answer quickly and completely, "Yes!"

Lord, we recognize that we are in danger of missing some really wonderful moments in life by refusing to allow ourselves to try again. Like Peter, we want to jump headfirst into Your grace, knowing that You will restore our hearts and reset our emotions. You are so kind, and we love You so much. In Jesus's name we pray. Amen.

I'm Not Keeping It from You to Tease You

Jesus Tells His Disciples to Wait for the Promise

What about now?"

I had promised my kids ice cream "a little later after lunch," and they kept coming into my office to see if it was time to eat it yet. "I'll get it in a little while," I answered them again and again. "You just finished lunch. Let's let that food settle before you put something else into your tummy."

This reasoning made absolutely no sense to them. "Why can't we just have it now?" they demanded to know. The truth is, I knew they'd be hungry before dinner, and I planned the ice cream as an afternoon snack to bridge the gap between lunch and supper. I had a good plan for them; it just wasn't time yet. Waiting can be the absolute worst.

Really, there's nothing I hate more than waiting and not knowing when something is going to happen. Give me a calendar with a date circled on it. Give me a time that my favorite show will come on TV. Give me something to hold on to. Just like my children, it feels like agony to wait for an undetermined moment to arrive.

But Scripture shows us that every good thing is worth waiting for. Noah waited over four hundred days to get off the boat. But the rain stopped and they were saved. Abraham waited twenty-five years for the son had God promised Him. But Isaac came and God fulfilled His word. Joseph waited decades to see his dream come to pass. But God remembered him and set him over Egypt. The world waited thousands of years for the promised Messiah, but Jesus came right on time. God keeps His words and He keeps His timing.

Right before Jesus ascended into heaven, He gave His disciples one final instruction. He said, "Do not leave Jerusalem, but wait for the gift my Father promised, which you have heard me speak about. For John baptized with water, but in a few days you will be baptized with the Holy Spirit."[129]

They weren't sure what this would look like. They didn't know exactly when it would take place, but they knew what God had promised. And just as He did with every other promise, God kept this one. He poured out His Holy Spirit, sending a Comforter to fill and lead the disciples in what they would do next.

We each pass through different seasons of waiting, but they are never wasted. They aren't pointless. They serve a purpose, because we spend time with the Lord differently when we are waiting for Him to do something. We experience an expectation that we don't have once the promise arrives. Our prayers, our praise, and our worship are all seasoned differently in times of waiting than they are when we are enjoying what the Lord has promised. So we have the opportunity to trust God while we're waiting for His word to be fulfilled in a way we won't ever get to trust Him again.

I don't know what you're waiting for. Another baby? A better job? More money? Reconciliation with a family member? Healing to come in your marriage? God to fulfill that dream He placed in your heart a decade ago?

We cannot control God's timing, but we can choose how we wait for His promises to come.

The best news is that they always do. God never told anyone to wait for a promise He wouldn't fulfill. So that thing you're holding on to? The hope of what's to come? It hasn't been forgotten by God. And while we might keep popping in front of Him, saying, "Is it time now, God? Can I have it now? Can I do it now? Can it be time for this to finally happen?" God gently reassures our hearts, *I haven't forgotten about you. I know what you want, and I also know what's best. I'm not keeping it from you to tease you. I'm not just interested in teaching you a lesson. I am interested in protecting My perfect purposes in your life. Everything I do for you is compelled by My love. It will come to pass. Your waiting isn't in vain. Let's spend some time together until the time for this next promise arrives.*

Lord, we don't want to be kids who demand, "Now! Give it to me now!" We want to be daughters who are so secure in the love of our Father that we will wait for what He says is best. God, help us learn the lessons You want to teach us in this season fully and quickly. We love getting to grow in You. In Jesus's name we pray. Amen.

I Have Already Seen This Moment

The Holy Spirit Speaks to Ananias

Acts 9

Today if I told you that God asked me to put the oil in my diaper bag before I left the house, you might think that He was talking about a certain essential oil. However, when God spoke these words to me nearly six years ago, He was talking about a small vial of oil I used to pray for people. In Scripture, oil is mentioned a number of times in connection with prayer and healing. Mark 6:12–13 details the disciples' ministry work, saying, "They went out and preached that people should repent. They drove out many demons and anointed many sick people with oil and healed them." James 5:14 says, "Is anyone among you sick? Let them call the elders of the church to pray over them and anoint them with oil in the name of the Lord." About eight years ago, I started carrying a small vial of oil just in case I needed to pray for someone.

So when I felt God saying to bring the oil, I thought perhaps I'd have the opportunity to put some on my hands and pray for someone's healing. I did not think that it would be my own son as he suffered from a life-threatening anaphylactic reaction.

But that's exactly what happened. Kolton was three and tried a bite of cashew butter for the first time. Within minutes he was gasping for breath. I raced him to the ER, and as we were waiting for the epinephrine shot and steroids to kick in, I heard the same voice that told me to bring the oil in my bag remind me that it was there.

I pulled it out and began to pray for Kolton. The medicine began to work, but peace came through prayer. When I realized that God had told me to put the oil into my bag that morning, I understood that He had seen this moment coming. I realized right then that everything would be okay, because God was not surprised that we were in the ER. He was the one who told me we'd need the oil.

In Acts 9, God told a man named Ananias, "Go to the house of Judas on Straight Street and ask for a man from Tarsus named Saul, for he is praying. In a vision he has seen a man named Ananias come and place his hands on him to restore his sight."[130]

You might think that after such clear direction from the Lord with names and addresses, Ananias jumped up and said, "Whatever you say, God! I'll go right now!" But that didn't happen.

Ananias answered, "But Lord."[131] Wasn't this Saul the man who had been imprisoning Christians? Wouldn't it be dangerous for Ananias to go speak to this man? Did God really mean what He had said?! Couldn't God see this was a foolish thing to ask Ananias to do?

Despite his questioning, Ananias listened to God, went to Saul, welcomed him into the family of God, and Saul's life was forever changed.

God knew that Saul's heart had been changed. God knew exactly what would happen when Ananias went to meet with Saul. God had seen the outcome before He even offered Ananias the chance to be obedient. And He has the same foresight in our lives. He asks us to do things because He loves us.

Sometimes God's instructions to us seem outrageous. Sometimes they're simple. Sometimes God just says, "Bring an extra water bottle to practice." Or "Encourage that other mom in the store." Or "Throw an extra change of clothes into the diaper bag."

But these promptings don't only prove to us that God speaks to us, they also prove to us that God sees what we can't. He sees everything that we will need before we need it. He sees the outcome of every situation before we reach it. And every word and every encouragement that God gives us reveals His love to guide our hearts and expand His kingdom.

Today, the Lord would say to us, *Trust that you hear My voice. You know it. You have felt Me with you. You aren't a stranger to My love. So when I lead you, follow. When I give directions, take them. When I invite you in, come. When I seem to delay, trust. When I say no, rejoice. When I say yes, press in. When I say wait, use the pause. And when I say I love you, believe it.*

Lord, thank You for being so involved in our lives that You don't only care about what's happening now; You know what's coming up ahead as well. I hear You reminding our hearts in this moment that You have it all figured out. We choose to follow You and be led even when we don't understand because You are a good shepherd. In Jesus's name we pray. Amen.

Notes

1. Genesis 1:26
2. Genesis 1:28
3. Hebrews 13:8
4. John 10:27, NASB
5. See Hebrews 4:12.
6. Genesis 3:1
7. Genesis 3:2–3
8. Genesis 3:7–9
9. Genesis 3:22
10. See Genesis 6–9.
11. Genesis 12:1–3
12. Genesis 19:17
13. Genesis 19:18–20
14. See Genesis 15–21.
15. Genesis 16: 11, 13
16. See Genesis 22:2.
17. Genesis 22:8
18. Genesis 22:12, 14
19. Genesis 25:23, NASB
20. Genesis 28:13–16
21. John 17:23
22. Genesis 35:11–12
23. Genesis 37:6–8
24. See Exodus 3:4–6.
25. Exodus 3:11
26. Exodus 3:12
27. Exodus 4:2
28. Exodus 4:3–5
29. See Exodus 3:12.
30. Exodus 4:1, 13
31. Exodus 4:14–17
32. Exodus 5:9
33. Exodus 6:6, 8
34. Exodus 6:9
35. Exodus 12:12
36. See Exodus 12:3, 7, 11, 13.
37. Exodus 12:31
38. Exodus 13:17
39. Exodus 14:15–16
40. Exodus 14:21–22
41. Exodus 16:31
42. Exodus 20:2
43. John 1:17
44. Joshua 6:2–5
45. See Philippians 4:6.
46. 1 Samuel 1:11
47. 1 Samuel 1:17
48. 1 Samuel 3:9
49. See 1 Kings 17:14–16.
50. 1 Kings 18:36, 38
51. 1 Kings 19:11–13
52. Numbers 22:20
53. Numbers 22:28, 31, 35
54. Numbers 23:8
55. See Romans 8:28.
56. Jonah 3:4
57. Jonah 3:10
58. Jonah 4:1–3
59. Jonah 4:4
60. Judges 6:12
61. Luke 1:35
62. Luke 1:38, BSB
63. Matthew 2:13

64. Matthew 3:14–15
65. Matthew 3:16–17
66. Matthew 3:17
67. John 14:27
68. Matthew 4:3–4
69. Matthew 4:10
70. 2 Corinthians 10:5
71. Luke 5:5
72. See Luke 5:6, 10.
73. John 1:47, NLT
74. John 1:48–49
75. See John 2:3–9.
76. Matthew 8:7–8, 10, 13, NKJV
77. Luke 7:37–38
78. Luke 7:48, 50
79. Luke 5:20
80. Luke 5:21
81. Luke 5:23
82. Luke 5:24–25
83. Luke 5:17, KJV
84. Luke 12:11–12
85. See Mark 4:37–40.
86. See Luke 8:44–48.
87. Matthew 14:28
88. Matthew 14:29
89. Matthew 14:31
90. John 5:19–20
91. Matthew 19:14
92. Matthew 15:32–37
93. Matthew 16:13–19
94. Luke 10:40–42
95. John 3:2
96. John 3:16–18
97. John 4:7
98. John 4:10
99. John 4:50–53
100. Mark 10:48–51, CEV
101. Mark 10:51, CEV
102. Mark 10:52, CEV
103. Luke 19:5–6
104. Luke 19:8–9
105. John 8:5–7
106. John 8:10–11
107. Matthew 20:21–22.
108. John 11:4–6
109. John 11:11–15
110. John 11:32–34
111. John 11:35
112. John 11:38
113. John 11:43
114. Matthew 26:10–12
115. John 13:4–5
116. John 13:8
117. John 13:8
118. Luke 22:31–34
119. John 14:15-18, NKJV
120. John 14:18
121. John 14:27
122. John 16:12–13
123. Luke 23:40–43
124. See John 20:13–16.
125. John 20:21, NASB
126. John 20:26–27, NASB
127. John 21:19
128. John 21:15
129. Acts 1:4–5
130. Acts 9:11–12
131. Acts 9:13, NLT